What others are saying about
Who Is My Neighbor?
How Will I Respond?

Connie Cole Jeske tells a story of love for a community and its people. The people of First United Methodist Church in Tulsa, Oklahoma, could hardly have known what God would make possible when they first engaged Eugene Field Elementary School. An effort that began to help others came to transform the lives of all involved. While they worked with few models to emulate, this book provides the many churches today seeking to engage their communities through schools both inspiration and examples to shed light upon their paths.
> —*Lovett Weems, Director, G. Douglass Lewis Center for Church Leadership*

Connie Jeske has somehow managed to redefine the meaning of how to be caregivers in today's culture! Scripturally based and expertly done, this book is a must read for every church and organization engaged in ministries to the poor and those in need.

Shaped by her own experiences of being part Cherokee and attending a predominately black school in Oklahoma during the desegregation of the 1970s, Connie was introduced to the concept of "justice" for the disenfranchised, and chronicles her lifelong advocacy of equality and legitimacy for everyone in this remarkable tapestry of stories and events.

I have been involved in ministry for more than forty-five years and I thought I knew something about caring for others—that is, until I read *Who Is My Neighbor?*
> —*Robert E. Hayes, Jr., Bishop, Oklahoma Area, The United Methodist Church*

It is almost impossible to quantify the impact that First United Methodist members have had on the students of Eugene Field Elementary. Their involvement included everything from endless hours of tutoring and mentoring to the sponsoring of school dinners for parents and the community and even the creation of a community grocery store. It was all about nurturing the whole child, and from that premise, Eugene Field became a model community school. That would not have been possible without the help of First United Methodist.

The depth of involvement by this caring community partner is 10 to the 1000th power, it is that powerful. The transformation that took place among the students, staff, and parents at this school would have been impossible without the help of First United Methodist. The partnership continues to this day.

—*Dr. Keith Ballard, former Tulsa School Superintendent*

On behalf of Halftimer Clark Millspaugh of First United Methodist Church, I endorse *Who Is My Neighbor?*. Connie Cole Jeske has led the efforts of Tulsa's First United Methodist Church in community ministries for more than twenty years. *Who Is My Neighbor?* is true to the spirit and mission of Halftime. Connie Jeske tells what it means to be a volunteer, how to lead volunteers, what is possible when faith and compassion merge, and perhaps most importantly, *why* to reach out to the needy. It is not only the needy who benefit, but the person who is serving. What a beautiful model our Lord has engineered for us. The givers with servant hearts and the receivers are both eternally blessed ... and along the way, needs are met and the world is made a better place!

—*Bob Buford, founder of The Halftime Institute*

As a church, we have found that loving our neighbor is messy, it's hard and it's wonderful. Connie Jeske tells the story of the people we have come to love and the lessons we have learned. We do not have a formula for ministry, but a narrative—and Connie presents that narrative honestly and winsomely in this book.

—*Dr. Wade Paschal, Senior Minister 2001-2016,*
First United Methodist Church Tulsa, OK

First United Methodist Church of Tulsa is a church that worships and serves with excellence. It is the same church when it is gathered or scattered. Its servant heart has been such for more than thirty years. In the initial weekend of *Motivation for Ministry*, clues for servant ministries were shared, principles given, and motivating stories of servant ministries told. Three hundred volunteers said, "Yes!"

Dr. Connie Cole Jeske has been the chief supervisor/champion of community ministries for more than twenty years, motivating the church and leading the servants. We are indebted to Dr. Jeske for this story she tells so well in this book about enabling ministries beyond the church walls.

As you read this book, many valuable details will be gained of how a church scattered can engage the culture around it. Read and rejoice at how a tutoring ministry at Eugene Field Elementary School led to adopting the school. Children have been taught better how to learn. Some have been enabled to go to college and are still supported with lasting friends. A new school building has been built and honors received from the Tulsa County and Oklahoma State Boards of Education.

There are a half dozen areas of ministry about which you will read with much reward. These are enduring ministries. This church knows how to fill and fulfill its servant hearts. Learning to identify needs calls forth new servants. The church and its servants continue to dream new dreams and birth new ventures.

God bless Tulsa First United Methodist Church and God bless the readers of these pages!

—Dr. James B. Buskirk, Senior Minister 1984-2001,
First United Methodist Church, Tulsa, OK

WHO IS *MY* NEIGHBOR?

HOW WILL I RESPOND?

Connie Cole Jeske

CJ²

Scripture references are from the New King James Version of the Bible unless otherwise designated. (Nashville, TN: Thomas Nelson Publishers)

Scripture quotations marked (ESV) are taken from The Holy Bible, English Standard Version Copyright © 2001 by Crossway Bibles, a publishing ministry of Good News Publishers.

Scripture quotations marked (NIV) are taken from the Holy Bible, New International Version®, NIV® Copyright ©1973, 1978, 1984, 2011 by Biblica, Inc.® Used by permission. All rights reserved worldwide.

ISBN 978-1517329471

Cover design by Julie Rains and Jennith Moncrief

Interior design by Jennifer Judson

Travis Hall Photography

To contact the author:
whoismyneighborbook1@gmail.com
www.Facebook.com/conniecolejeske

TO

Leroy Jeske
my best friend and husband
with gratitude for his unending love and support

and to
my First United Methodist Church family
The Lord knows the service you have given
in His name … and He is pleased!

and in memory of
Lori Rickman (1964–2013)
Emily Renberg (1947–2012)
Clark Millspaugh (1953–2012)
Clydella Hentschel (1936–2012)

Because of their service to the Lord,
I stand on their shoulders and see further
than I could if I had not known them.

Foreword

One Sunday morning, a church visitor at the early worship service at First United Methodist Church in Tulsa checked the box on the visitor card: "I would like a visit from a pastor." Her name was Lori. When we met at her apartment the Friday after her visit, I learned how deeply wounded Lori's life had been. I also learned that she was living with a person who had changed her life, someone who had loved her unconditionally, someone who had invited Lori into a new life. That day, Lori said, "You've got to meet my roommate!" That roommate was Connie Cole Jeske. When Connie and I met, it didn't take long to see that she was a woman of deep faith and conviction. As she chronicled her story with Lori, I knew that I had found a ministry partner and colleague, someone who saw the world the same way I did. My title at the time was Minister of Community Ministries. My job description was to "mobilize members in ministry beyond the walls of the church." When it came time to recommend a person to follow me in the position, it was clear that God had connected Connie to the life of our church for this purpose. In this powerful book, you will get a glimpse into the life of one who has given her all for the Kingdom of God in creative and specific ways. She gets it. She gets it in ways that all Christians need to get it. Her book is both inspiring and instructive. May Holy Spirit creativity come upon you as you read.

Rev. Jessica Moffatt
Senior Minister
First United Methodist Church, Tulsa, OK

Preface

First United Methodist Church Tulsa has a rich history of service—in the church, in the community, on faraway global mission fields—wherever members find themselves, they are equipped and energized to serve. When Dr. James Buskirk became senior pastor at First Methodist in 1984, God was about to move in a dramatic way, calling the church to new levels of servant ministry and into new, never-been-done-before, innovative outreaches. Dr. Buskirk was a pioneer in motivating and mobilizing laity to serve. I am grateful for his leadership, creativity, and guidance, and for challenging me to dream bigger dreams and think beyond the tried and conventional. The combination of his encouragement and my desire to see transformation in a community was the catalyst for First United Methodist Church Tulsa making the commitment to adopt nearby Eugene Field Elementary School.

Who Is My Neighbor? grew out of a threefold desire to document the stories of FUMC members who share their lives and faith daily, to tell a part of the FUMC Tulsa story, and to share the valuable insights for ministry that we have learned.

As we have intentionally served outside the walls of our church, we are grateful for the work of so many who have led the way in community development. I am grateful to Steve Corbett and Brian Fikkert for their challenge to us in *When Helping Hurts: How to Alleviate Poverty Without Hurting the Poor—and Yourself* as well as John Perkins and Bob Lupton.

Many people have contributed to this book and I am grateful for their gifts. I want to thank Morgan Cunningham, Carol McCoy, John and Shelli Pleasant, Jennifer Judson, Joshua Danker-Dake, Nancy Kirby, June Autry, and the staff, students and community of Eugene Field Elementary School.

I also want to thank my mother, Louise Cole, and my amazing family, Rick, Pam, Court, Ryan, Penelope, Elisha, Melissa, Sydney, Joshua, Michaela, Zoe, River, Asher, and Hannah.

Table of Contents

"My grace is sufficient for you, for my
power is made perfect in weakness."
(2 Corinthians 12:9 NIV)

"He has shown you, O man,
what is good;
And what does the LORD
require of you
But to do justly,
To love mercy,
And to walk humbly with your God?"
(Micah 6:8)

1

Caregiving

Caregiving is not complicated.

We see a need.

We care about the person who has the need.

We act to meet the need in the best way we know.

Our problem is not with the basics of the process.

Rather, our problem with caregiving is with the details—which person or group of people to help, and which methods or protocols to follow in seeking to meet as much need as possible with maximum use of available time, energy, skills, and material resources.

Aha!

Caregiving becomes complicated the minute we start doing it!

And beyond those basics, there are all sorts of organizational issues that seem to arise: who will do what, and when, and where, and with what percentage of the available budget, and at what level of priority? How will we know when we have done enough, and more importantly, how will we know when the Lord sees our "mission" as being accomplished?

We do well to seek answers to three questions:

One, *who* is our neighbor?

Two, *how* do we wrap our arms around that person or group of people?

Three, *what* is our personal individual responsibility and role in the caregiving?

Jesus gave us clear direction in answering each of these questions.

.

2

A Challenge and Its Context

Let's dive in deep.

Nearly every challenge, experience, and commitment we make in life can be understood best in the context of the motivations that give rise to it. When we ask "Why?" and come to an answer, we nearly always face a follow-up question, "What now?" And when that question is answered, we have a mandate for action.

For many years, we at First United Methodist Church (FUMC) in Tulsa, Oklahoma, have been asking "Why?" about many issues and needs. The question always brings us to the "What now?" question, and the answer to that question is virtually always, "because God said."

The variations on God's message may be, "because the Bible commands this," or "because Jesus taught this," or "because we sense the Holy Spirit compelling us to …" Unless there's a divine why, there's not much reason to act.

This is a book about caregiving and, specifically, about the various ministries we have pursued for the last thirty years as a church body to care for members in our church and our greater community as the "hands and feet of Christ Jesus." We have more than twenty community-based caregiving initiatives every year at First United Methodist, with several hundred members involved in them. The ministries are diverse, some of them short-lived and some longstanding. They are exciting, challenging, and, for the most part, perceived by those who receive our care as beneficial and desirable. From the perspective of the clergy, the ministries are a vital way in which the members of this church grow spiritually and find increased fulfillment in their lives. We eagerly seek to have a vibrant outreach ministry that will have many more facets and involve many more. We aspire to see more lay people involved in outreach to our neighborhood and the world. But we rejoice in what has been and what is.

Our story has a history, and many practical examples of things to do and not to do. This book will relate a number of those. But at the heart of our purpose is the *why* question and its answers. For you to understand more fully what we have done, we will start with *why*.

An Extension of What Jesus Did

From what the Scriptures tell us in the tenth chapter of the gospel of Luke, the day described was a joy-filled day in the earthly life and ministry of Jesus and His followers. Jesus had sent out seventy of His close followers, two by two, telling them to take no money, knapsack, or sandals, and to greet no one along the road—rather, to go into a village and say to the first house they entered, "Peace to this house."

If the household extended hospitality, the disciples were to stay with that family and heal the sick and preach the good news of Jesus' ministry in that town and make that house their headquarters. If the disciples were not received with hospitality in a village, they were to move on, shaking the dust from their feet. Jesus pronounced punishment on those who refused to hear His message and receive His followers.

The day we focus on here is the day the disciples *return*.

What a great report they have to give!

They say with joy, "Lord, even the demons are subject to us in Your name." Jesus rejoices with them, encouraging them to keep their focus on the truth that their names were written in heaven, not that they had power over all things evil. In that same hour, however, we also read that Jesus Himself rejoiced in the Spirit, saying, "I thank You, Father, Lord of heaven and earth, that You have hidden these things from the wise and prudent and revealed them to babes. Even so, Father, for so it seemed good in Your sight. All things have been delivered to Me by My Father, and no one knows who the Son is except the Father, and who the Father is except the Son, and the one to whom the Son wills to reveal Him."

Then Jesus turns to His disciples and says, "Blessed are the eyes which see the things you see; for I tell you that many prophets and kings have desired to see what you see, and have not seen it, and to hear what you hear, and have not heard it."

The next thing that happens seems startling, for it does not appear to be within the context of this joy-filled reporting of spiritual victory. The Bible tells us, "Behold, a certain lawyer stood up and tested Him, saying, 'Teacher, what shall I do to inherit eternal life?'"

Jesus answers, "What is written in the law? What is your reading of it?"

The lawyer—who practiced religious law for religious leaders—says, "'You shall love the Lord your God with all your heart, with all your soul, with all your strength, and with all your mind,' and 'your neighbor as yourself.'"

Jesus replies, "You have answered rightly; do this and you will live."

And then we come to the heart of the matter. The lawyer, "wanting to justify himself," says to Jesus, "And who is my neighbor?"

The answer Jesus gives him will be something we analyze closely, but before we get ahead of ourselves, let me point out several key points related to what happened on this day.

First, Jesus sent out His followers to be an extension of Himself—to display His love, compassion, healing power, and authority. These seventy disciples were to be *among* the people as they gave His messages about the kingdom of God. They were to give freely and to honor their hosts by remaining loyal to them. They were *not* sent to display top-down authority, but rather to be the purveyors of ministry in a role-modeling, peer-to-peer manner.

They were not priests. Those sent out by Jesus were not theologically trained in any formal way. They had simply spent time with Jesus and had watched Him model before them an exciting way of believing and living.

Jesus called upon them to heal the people and extend "good news," or encouragement. There is a wonderful message in that mission statement since healing nearly always brings about encouragement, and in many cases, encouragement produces a healing or therapeutic effect.

There must also be an understanding on our part that healing covers so much more than physical recovery from natural diseases or injuries. Jesus was asking His followers to copy *His* ministry—which He understood clearly in terms presented centuries before by the prophet Isaiah:

> "The Spirit of the Lord God is upon Me,
>
> Because the Lord has anointed Me to preach good tidings to the poor;
>
> He has sent Me to heal the brokenhearted,
>
> To proclaim liberty to the captives, and the opening of the prison to those who are bound;
>
> To proclaim the acceptable year of the Lord, and the day of vengeance of our God;
>
> To comfort all who mourn,
>
> To console those who mourn in Zion,
>
> To give them beauty for ashes, the oil of joy for mourning, the garment of praise for the spirit of heaviness; that they may be called trees of righteousness, the planting of the Lord, that He may be glorified."
> (Isaiah 61:1–3)

If we are to reflect Jesus to our world, we do well to focus on these very attributes:

- *Preach good tidings*—Stay focused on what Jesus said and did.

- *Heal the brokenhearted*—Be a fountain of encouragement and faith, carrying the message that no problem or situation is beyond the control and power of God to create a remedy.

- *Proclaim liberty to the captives*—Engage in a ministry that produces deliverance from all of the snares of evil.

- *Open the prison to those who are bound*—Voicing that freedom is possible from the bondage of sin; it is possible to walk in freedom and purity as the Spirit empowers us and to live in reconciliation with God the Father.

- *Proclaim the acceptable year of the Lord, and the day of vengeance of our God*—To express clearly the truth that today is the day that the Lord desires to save the lost and the truth that there is a day of final reckoning and divine judgment coming that cannot be escaped.

- *Comfort all who mourn*—First and foremost, mourning their sin and the consequences of rebellion against God, consoling especially those who consider themselves to be God's people but are suffering in the wake of sinful decisions made by their leaders.

- *Give a renewed sense of hope*—What is decaying and dead might once again be fruitful and alive, to lead the people in praise and the pursuit of deep inner joy that comes from a relationship with the Lord, and to give the people a glimpse of how the Lord sees their future: as evergreen trees of righteousness that will bring glory to God.

If we only do that, we have done a great deal!

It should also be noted that Isaiah went on to say that it was not the Messiah or "preacher" who would bring about amazing changes among the people; rather, it was the people themselves who heard and heeded the anointed message of the Lord. They were the ones who would "rebuild the old ruins," "raise up the former desolations," "repair the ruined cities," and experience tremendous prosperity in their flocks and vineyards (see Isaiah 61:4–7). The call to the people was that they might truly become the servants of God and receive *all* of the honor God desired for them.

What a powerful word to the people in Old Testament days, and to *us*!

It certainly was a powerful word as spoken by the seventy followers of Jesus sent out to preach His message of reconciliation to masses that had been largely ignored and maligned by the religious power structure of Jerusalem.

This book is about reaching out to those in our communities that we perceive to be in need—not only material need, but emotional, educational, and spiritual poverty. The most powerful gifts we can give are those Isaiah identified:

encouragement, faith, deliverance from sin, healing that leads to wholeness, truth, hope, and comfort. This does not discount or dismiss our need to give very practical aid to the needy—including material resources, educational opportunity, and a political voice and justice. Rather, it is a claim that material, educational, and political assistance *alone* do not address the fullness of human need. The church is uniquely positioned to offer a whole-person approach to development and a future that is better than the present or past.

Second, Jesus and the disciples were excited about two different things, or so it seems. The disciples returned with wonder and excitement that the demons had been subject to their use of the Lord's name. Their focus was on the flow of power they had experienced in their lives and the results they had witnessed— very likely the casting out of many demons and the healing of diseased bodies.

Jesus replied to them in what seems to be a very matter-of-fact manner. He told them that He had given them the authority to trample on serpents and scorpions, and over all the power of the enemy. In other words, He seemed to indicate that He expected this result. (In Scripture, serpents are usually a symbol of evil power and scorpions a symbol of the "stinging" and sometimes deadly actions of evil people.)

What is it that truly excited Jesus to voice His excitement in praise and thanksgiving to His Heavenly Father? Jesus was pleased that His followers had been blessed to see God at work and that their names were written in heaven. Their work validated *His* work, and therefore, their work brought the highest blessings of God to their lives.

While Jesus no doubt was pleased that so many people had been healed and delivered by the activities of His disciples, done in His name and by His authority, He was *more* pleased at the work that the Spirit of God had done in His followers. The missionary excursion into the towns and villages of Galilee was ultimately for the benefit of Jesus' *disciples*—they were the ones most blessed.

The missionary excursion into the towns and villages of Galilee was ultimately for the benefit of Jesus' *disciples*—they were the ones most blessed.

We see this all the time among caregivers, teachers, preachers, social workers, and others who engage in a wide variety of healing arts and sciences. The one doing the caregiving, teaching, preaching, and so forth is the one *most* blessed and the one who reaps the greatest intangible rewards that not only last a lifetime but have the potential to extend into eternity. We can never adequately measure our "success" in meeting the needs of the poor if we limit ourselves to economic factors and job growth, numbers of people involved, served, or benefited, or factors related to the modernization or remodeling of buildings and facilities. The intangibles are where the real results are achieved. We do not sacrifice one type of result for the other—true helping is a both/and endeavor.

What we must recognize is that God's agenda for our helping and need-meeting is often different than our own. While we desire to serve the Lord in what we do, the Lord desires to change and develop us through the process.

Third, the people in Jesus' day lived in different social strata, not unlike people today. The religious leaders, including the "certain lawyer" who questioned Jesus, were part of a group that perceived itself to be at the top of the heap. They had intellect, wealth, tradition, position, and religious systems on their side. They had a strong belief that they deserved these positive benefits to a great extent because of what they had done: they had studied the law (Torah) and obeyed not only the Scriptures but all of the hundreds of laws that had been developed by religious authorities through the centuries.

With their lofty view of themselves, those who were among the religious elite had a disdain for the uneducated and poor, who they believed had also "earned" their lowly status through their neglect of religious traditions and commandments and their lack of routine participation in attending synagogue services. The religious elite had a tremendous dislike for the people who did not live up to their standards of purity and rule-keeping. They called them "the people of the dirt"—just as might be thought today, that was about as low a criticism as could be levied.

The lawyer who comes to Jesus asks a question intended to put Jesus on the spot. The Bible tells us he stands up to "test" Jesus, asking, "What shall I do to inherit eternal life?"

Jesus asks him how he interpreted the Law. The man replies by quoting the very heart of the Law—a set of statements from Deuteronomy 6:5 and Leviticus 19:18.

> "You shall love the LORD your God with all your heart,
> with all your soul, with all your strength, and with all your
> mind, and your neighbor as yourself."

Elsewhere in the New Testament, Jesus stated publicly that these statements were a good summary of *all* the Law and the Prophets. Certainly, to devote oneself to the keeping of these two commands would take all of one's effort on any given day.

These commands, while stated succinctly and simply, are not simple—it is one thing to understand the concepts as they relate to *what* is being required and another thing to know *how* to keep the commands and *apply* the concepts. How does a person love the Lord with all his or her heart, soul, strength, and mind? Keeping the prescribed rituals and obeying God's commands are certainly part of that, but how can this obedience to ritual and command be identified, prioritized, and *measured*? *By whom? And with what categorization or degree of reward?* Implementation of obedience is a complicated matter!

Discussing these commands could take weeks, not minutes. Jesus seems to assume that the lawyer is capable of sorting out the answer for himself ... if he chooses to do so.

The lawyer, however, seeks to "justify himself"—in other words, to get Jesus to agree that a true neighbor is a person who *also* seeks to love the Lord with all his heart, soul, mind, and strength.

Can you see where this leads? It leads to the strong helping the strong, the smart helping the smart, the godly helping the godly, the rich helping the rich, the spiritually mature helping the spiritually maturing. It leads to a person being required to "get good" before that person can "get God." It leads to a person being required to come to church—and usually to attend and join that church—in order to be allowed to participate fully in the life of that church. It leads to a spiritual division between those worthy of the gospel and those who must follow a set of procedures and regulations to *become* worthy.

If this lawyer could get Jesus to agree that many of the people the disciples had delivered, healed, or encouraged were unqualified or undeserving of deliverance, healing, or encouragement, he would have scored a major debate point over Jesus and dismissed the ministry of the disciples as errant.

That may be the reason that Jesus said to His disciples what He said—He knew this man and his critical question were waiting in the wings. Jesus wanted His disciples to be affirmed that their ministry did not depend on what those who were helped said or did in the wake of their ministry. The Lord was pleased and His rewards were eternal.

There are two important principles for us to see today as we embark on ministry to our neighbors, principles related to *respect* and *expected return*.

Respect. The first principle has this as its central question: *"Do we respect fully those who are going to receive our ministry?"* Or do we see them as "lesser than" individuals who may not fully deserve what we have to give, or who may not have the capacity or proclivity to value what we give? Do we seek to minister to the needy because we think it is a "good thing" to do or because others around us think we are a good person to engage in a particular outreach? Or do we engage in outreach because we know God has sent us out to do His work and that He alone determines the results and the rewards?

Expected Return. The second principle is addressed by this question: *"What do we expect in return from those we serve?"* Do we expect them to come to our church? Do we expect them to adopt our culture and to begin to dress, act, and talk as we do? Do we expect them to be exceedingly, abundantly grateful … or at least be a *little* thankful?

These two sets of questions are good to ponder if we seek to be part of an outreach to people in need. How we see ourselves and others and what we expect of others are two critical issues to address.

Marching Orders from What Jesus Said

It is interesting to me that Jesus does not directly answer the lawyer's question, "Who is my neighbor?"

Instead, He tells a story that becomes "marching orders" for all of Jesus' followers after that day.

Jesus says,

> "A certain man went down from Jerusalem to Jericho, and fell among thieves, who stripped him of his clothing, wounded him, and departed, leaving him half dead. Now by chance a certain priest came down that road. And when he saw him, he passed by on the other side. Likewise a Levite, when he arrived at the place, came and looked and passed by on the other side. But a certain Samaritan, as he journeyed, came where he was. And when he saw him, he had compassion. So he went to him and bandaged his wounds, pouring on oil and wine; and he set him on his own animal, brought him to an inn, and took care of him. On the next day, when he departed, he took out two denarii, gave them to the innkeeper, and said to him, 'Take care of him; and whatever more you spend, when I come again, I will repay you.' So which of these three do you think was neighbor to him who fell among the thieves?" (Luke 10:30–36)

The road between Jerusalem and Jericho was notoriously dangerous. The road was very steep. Jerusalem was and is built on the top of a mountain range; Jericho is below sea level along the Jordan River to the east. The ancient road linking the two cities had many twists and turns—switchbacks—and was often bordered by a drop-off cliff and deep ravine, all in the space of about fifteen miles. Accidents with carts and donkeys were common as loads tended to shift precariously and the dirt road was subject to deep ruts that made footing unsure for both animals and humans. Furthermore, animals of prey lived in the caves and crevices on both sides of the road. "Men of prey" also took advantage of the dangerous route. They could spring seemingly from nowhere to rob travelers and then disappear as quickly as they came. Lone travelers were most susceptible to danger.

Those who traveled the road were usually traders and priests. Families and more casual travelers took other routes. Those going north often took the mountain road along the crest of the mountain range.

Jericho was a major suburb for priests and their families. The priests who served in the temple did so according to prescribed shifts. At the time of Jesus, the priests who were assigned to serve in Herod's temple traveled into the heart of Jerusalem and lived in the rooms built for them under the Temple Mount. They served in shifts of two weeks or longer depending on their seniority and job—doing such things as baking the shewbread, preparing the incense, keeping sufficient olive oil on hand and enough wicks for the great menorah, tending the robes of the high priest, overseeing the use of the baptismal pools used for ritual cleansing, sacrificing the animals and birds brought to the temple altars, and assisting in a wide variety of ceremonial and practical chores related to their personal lives and the lives of those who received assistance from the temple (such as those granted official status as widows).

The priests who lived in Jericho were usually eager to get home at the end of a shift, and for the most part, they did not have much in the way of possessions, and they were therefore not susceptible to robbery.

Tradesmen who used the Jericho Road tended to be those who were on their way to meet with a caravan traveling on the eastern edge of the mountains in the Jordan River Valley. It is very likely that the man who was robbed had been such a trader. The robbers had taken whatever animal or cart he may have been using, had stripped him of his clothing, and had badly wounded him, perhaps thinking they had actually killed him.

Jesus notes in His story that a priest comes by and walks by the wounded man, staying as far away from him as possible. The priest may have assumed the man was dead, and to touch a dead person would have rendered the priest ceremonially unclean. This would have been especially problematic if the priest was on his way *to* the temple rather than returning to Jericho. We don't know from Jesus' story which way the priest is going, although most people assume the phrase "going down the road" refers to a literal descent. What we do know is that he passes by without stopping, apparently not even going close enough to the person to determine that he *was* a person or whether he was still alive.

11

Next along the road is a Levite—a descendant of the priestly tribe but who is not working as a priest. He may have been part of the overall religious bureaucracy, perhaps even a "lawyer" such as the man who questioned Jesus. Levites were considered aristocratic, law-abiding, and concerned with ceremony, custom, and keeping their distance from anything considered suspect. This man pauses to look, concludes that there is nothing he could or should do, and moves on.

Finally, Jesus says a third traveler comes by. Jesus describes him as a Samaritan, a member of a group of people who were known as "half-breeds" and who lived in an area northeast of Jerusalem and northwest of Jericho. The Samaritans in ancient centuries had been members of the northern Israelite tribes who had intermarried with invading Assyrians—either going to Assyria and later returning or marrying with the Assyrians who were sent to live in northern Israel. Other invading groups of people also tended to intermarry with those who settled in Samaria. The Jews had no regard for these distant cousins and refused to allow them access to Jewish holy places or participation in Jewish rituals.

This traveler, the most unlikely person in Jesus' story, stops to do what he can for the man who has been robbed.

It is important to note several things at this point in the story.

First, the Samaritan did not know whether the man was dead or alive, or if there was anything that might be done to help him. He really didn't know anything about the man's age, race, status, or overall condition. He made it his mission to get answers. That is a critically important consideration for those who seek to help people they perceive as needy.

We must approach any needy person or group with an eye toward the greatest number and types of opportunities to help them. Even if we cannot help them personally or as a volunteer group, this does not mean that we cannot become an agent for getting them valuable assistance.

We must ask:

Who are they, and in what ways might their race, culture, or age determine the ways in which they can be helped?

How are they needy?

In *what ways* might they be helped with needs that may not be obvious?

These questions are worthy to be asked and answered not as a matter of prejudice or preferential treatment, but in sincere awareness that some forms of help are made available in our world to people because of their specific age, race, or culture. At times, we seem so intent on the limitations of certain types of aid that we overlook a vast number of opportunities for "free" help made available through private agencies, foundations, and very specific secular programs. In Oklahoma, for example, a wide variety of programs are designated exclusively for those who have American Indian heritage—and among these are very fine healthcare programs, educational scholarships, and career training opportunities, some of which are offered for American Indians of all heritages and others by specific tribes. Many of these programs are funded by the tribes, not the federal or state government.

Second, the Samaritan was willing to use what he personally had available to help the man to the degree he could. As one colleague of mine once said about this story: He gave generously out of his own saddlebag.

If we take an inventory of what this Samaritan had to offer, we see that he had a donkey, very likely a second tunic or garment, wine, and oil. These were not uncommon travel items at that time. As part of his garments, the Samaritan may have had strips of cloth that were often taken on trips for use in creating slings and bandages. Any person who has traveled in the Middle East is aware that cuts, scrapes, twisted ankles, blisters, wounds from falls, and other injuries related to simple walking and climbing are commonplace. Wine (even in vinegar form) can serve as a nonperishable disinfectant and can help an injured person with pain. Oil serves as a helpful balm in bandaging and cleansing a wound.

The point here is that virtually every person has something he or she can do or give to help a person who is truly needy. It may be nothing more than a shoulder to cry on. It may be a ride on one's donkey—in our world, vehicle—to a nearby clinic, shelter, or place that distributes food. It may be the use of a cell phone to call for emergency aid. There's nearly always something practical that can be given.

I have a friend who carries a small wooden cross in the glove compartment of her car. It is designed to fit nicely in the palm of the hand. She said, "I have given these to several people, who also have placed these crosses in their cars. Two of my friends had occasion to stop at an accident scene and give a cross to an injured person—one placed the cross into the hand of a person even as she prayed for him and waited with him for an ambulance to arrive. It is such a simple act of love and care—and of faith and hope. If we do nothing more for a person in need, we can certainly stop to pray and to offer a word of encouragement."

In the story Jesus told, there was no spiritual activity offered by the Samaritan, but from all we know about basic human nature in times of crisis, I have no doubt that this Samaritan was praying for wisdom and for the ability to help, even if his prayer was silent.

Surely this is something all caregivers can and *must* do—prayer may very well be the only thing we can do, but in many cases, it is the *best* thing we can do, and from the vantage point of eternity, may be the most *effectual* thing we can do.

Third, the Samaritan surely must have recognized the potential for danger to himself. This man by the side of the road had been beaten up and robbed, which would have been evidence to any person passing that way that this was a dangerous stretch of road. Alternatively, the man lying by the side of the road may have been a decoy, with robbers waiting just beyond the nearest big rocks and bushes. The Samaritan did not let the thought of danger keep him from doing what he could for a person in need. He may have had one eye on alert for potential trouble, but he kept binding the wounds in earnest.

How many times in our world do we hear people say, "I was afraid to do anything. The situation seemed dangerous. And even if it wasn't dangerous, in this day and age, I could have been sued for doing the wrong thing or for not doing enough!"

Not everybody can help in medical or other practical ways that might involve physical strength or agility, and we must be wise in the kind and degree of help we offer. But I feel confident that every genuine victim or person in genuine need *wants* help and that every person who desires to give help can do *something*. We must be generous in giving the help we can give. We must also be willing to activate our own faith to overcome our fears related to helping.

Jesus says in the story that the Samaritan put the injured man on his donkey and continued on his way to Jericho, where he paid the innkeeper there to provide lodging and food for him for two days. The amount of money offered by the Samaritan was the average fee for two days' worth of minimum-wage labor at that time. He further offered to pay any additional charges when he returned that way.

There must have been something about this Samaritan that made him trustworthy in the eyes of the innkeeper—surely his example of helping would have also made him an example of goodness in humanity.

One thing that Jesus omits in the story is any response from the man who was robbed and wounded. The Samaritan certainly cared about what happened to this man—evident by his paying for his care—but he did not exact any repayment or indicate that the wounded man owed him so much as a "thank you."

What a good thing for us to remember as we address the needs of people we encounter: we may never be praised, thanked, or even acknowledged for the help we offer! The people we help may not be appreciative. Even so, we are called to be role models of good caregiving. Jesus made it very clear that He desired for His followers to be proactive in their giving and caring, without consideration of repayment or reward. (See Luke 6:38 and note that those who receive for their giving do not necessarily receive from those to whom they give.)

Finally, this Samaritan did not go looking for a wounded traveler to help. He did not seek out an opportunity to be a compassionate caregiver. Rather, he responded out of the compassion in his heart to a need that was in his way.

We do not need to go out looking for people to help. God will put them in our path. We do not need to scout out need. It is all around us. As one person said to me not long ago, "Most of us have to go out of our way and do our best to look away and close our ears to keep from encountering need."

Four Key Principles that Frame Caregiving

In my experience, our caregiving is ultimately framed by these four principles:

- *God puts the needy in our path.* He has put the needy in our neighborhood, whether individually or as a group. We don't need to seek them out—but we *do* need to open our eyes and see them in our midst.

- *God has given us an ability to help the needy that He puts in our path.* He has given us the talents and resources to do *something* to alleviate their need, to help them to the best of our ability to resolve their own problems to the best of *their* ability.

- *God does not choose us to be caregivers because of our educational qualifications or skills or because we are exactly like the people we help.* There are no prerequisites for the "type" of person worthy of our care or aid. Nor is there a profile of the ideal volunteer caregiver. God can use any person who is *willing* to give what he or she can give to help meet a need.

- *God will usually involve more than one person in giving care or assistance to a needy person.* The Samaritan became something of a caregiving team in association with the innkeeper in Jericho. The Lord expects us to work together in meeting needs—it is His organizational plan! The backdrop for this story of the Samaritan also reveals that principle—Jesus sent out His followers *two by two* to do His ministry and bring focus to the good news of His love, healing, and message of spiritual reconciliation.

We are admonished by Jesus, "Freely you have received, freely give" (Matt. 10:8).

The Lawyer's Response to the Story

After Jesus tells His story, He asks the lawyer, "Which of these three do you think was neighbor to him who fell among the thieves?"

The answer, of course, is obvious, and the lawyer has little choice but to reply, "He who showed mercy on him." In other words, the one who actually did something in an attempt to help. For many people, mercy is an emotion or an "intention." For Jesus and the people of His day, it was a *deed*, something actually done. Jesus responds to the lawyer, "Go and do likewise."

And that settles the issue. The conversation is over, the answer fully given.

And Then …

It is interesting to me that the very next story told in Luke's gospel is Jesus' visit to the home of a woman named Martha. In her desire to be a good hostess to Jesus, she becomes preoccupied with fixing and serving a fine feast for Him and His close disciples. Martha's sister, Mary, sits at the feet of Jesus, hanging on every word He spoke (see Luke 10:38–42).

Martha becomes perturbed and says, "Lord, do You not care that my sister has left me to serve alone? Therefore tell her to help me." Jesus replies, "Martha, Martha, you are worried and troubled about many things. But one thing is needed, and Mary has chosen that good part, which will not be taken away from her."

This passage may seem totally unrelated to the story of the Samaritan who helped the man who had been beaten and robbed. I see them as directly related.

Both the Samaritan and Martha were people motivated to care for others, and further, to share what they possessed with others. The Samaritan was generous with his time, effort, and possessions. Martha was generous, too, with her home and material resources.

It appears, however, that the Samaritan was motivated by *compassion* in his service to the injured man (see Luke 10:33). Martha, in contrast, seems to have been motivated by *a sense of duty or obligation*.

The Samaritan doesn't think twice in stopping to help the wounded man. Martha thinks of nothing else but her obligation to be a good hostess.

The Samaritan is focused outward, apparently with little regard for his personal safety or for any recognition or social reward. Martha is focused inward—very much concerned with how her meal is to be cooked, served, and enjoyed, and also about her ongoing reputation with Jesus and His followers.

The implications for volunteer service to people in need are profound.

Jesus calls us to be motivated by genuine compassion, which goes beyond sympathy for the suffering of others into the realm of true empathy. Compassion is not a mere emotion, although it has an emotional component. It is a clarion inner compulsion to *do* something, to act on behalf of the needy person and to offer whatever assistance is required to alleviate an abiding problem or pain. Compassion is always *other*-centered. Furthermore, it is *people*-focused.

Jesus did not elaborate in His story by referring to any thought process in those who saw the wounded traveler. We don't know with certainty, but one or more of them may very well have said, "Oh my, another victim along this dangerous road. We really must do something to ensure the safety of travelers; perhaps hire armed guards to accompany travelers. Or launch a greater effort to find, arrest, and punish robbers." While these are good concerns to have in the broader realms of social justice, they are not identified by Jesus as a cause for offering assistance to people or, more specifically, to a *person* in need. Biblical compassion is not issue-focused—it is always directed *from* the heart of the Lord *through* the heart of a caregiver *to* the heart of a person in need.

Biblical compassion is always directed *from* the heart of the Lord *through* the heart of a caregiver *to* the heart of a person in need.

Jesus says to Martha, "One thing is needed, and Mary has chosen that good part, which will not be taken away from her." (Luke 10:42) And what was that "one necessary thing"? It was a desire to have such a close relationship with Jesus that at every opportunity, she would put herself into position to hear His every word, and then act on it.

That must be our deepest desire, too.

3

The Helpful Servant

A friend of mine says of her fellow nurses: "A caregiver is a caregiver is a *caregiver*. Good hands-on nurses are always good caregivers. It doesn't matter if they have one patient or a dozen."

I find that also true in the best volunteer helpers regardless of their profession or background. They are caring individuals in every area of life, and they are good caregivers to one recipient or to many. They don't need an audience to perceive an opportunity to be the hands and feet of Christ.

I routinely encourage people to look at their lives and ask, "How has the Lord been working?" The more we look, the more we find His leading and His desire for us to become a servant to others.

Today, much of my work as a member of the clergy is very task oriented, but at my heart, I have been and am a caregiver to people. I do not see myself as serving the "church" as a whole—although I certainly desire to do that—but rather as serving individual people and groups who make up the church.

The caregiver that I know the most about is myself. That is true for every caregiver, of course. While I was initially reluctant to use my own life story in this book, much less relate it to the parable of the Good Samaritan, I was admonished by several people to step up to the plate. I offer you these next few pages as a possible mirror for appreciating the way God has been at work preparing you for more active caregiving, or for preparing you to lead a caregiving ministry. There are threads of lessons learned in my life that I have seen in the lives of many who have been longstanding lay servants at First United Methodist—different applications but very similar principles. If you see yourself in my story, then I am pleased that I was talked into this degree of personal vulnerability! If your experience has been different than mine—I rejoice in that. At minimum, I trust that you will benefit from examining the question, "How has the Lord brought me to this place and time?"

In his book *Invitation to a Journey*, Robert Mulholland, Jr., wrote that spiritual formation is a "process of being conformed to the image of Christ for the sake of others." Truly we *all* are in "spiritual formation"! The people and methods God uses may differ, but the end result is the same: *we become genuine servants of our Lord.*

How Has the Lord Been Working?

I truly believe I was wired from birth to be a caregiver. My undergraduate degree was in nursing, my master's degree in counseling, and my doctorate in ministry. Even today, in an administrative pastoral role, I find myself most fulfilled when I am involved in caregiving—it is a fulfilling of my life's purpose.

There are three major factors in my personal life that contributed to the work I do today and about which I feel tremendous passion.

Each of those factors has a name: *Booker T., Jesus,* and *Lori.*

I could easily write this book and present many of my ideas without even mentioning Booker T. and Lori. I probably could not write without mentioning Jesus. But my reason for telling you about all three of these influencing factors in more than a cursory way is because each created a dimension of caregiving in me that I believe to be important for any volunteer or caregiver to have, even in small doses.

Booker T. gave me a window of insight into social justice, and I still have a deep inclination to seek out social justice seminars and to discover new ways of helping the disenfranchised—to bring greater economic opportunities and greater access to genuine democratic political and legal equality.

Jesus and my conversion to becoming a follower of Jesus Christ in early years—gave me an inside awareness and conviction that I am commanded to live out a purpose of service to others. Even if a person does not sense that he or she has an innate, intuitive servant's heart, as a follower of Jesus, that person is commanded by Jesus to *serve.* It's also true that the more a person serves, the more the heart to serve seems to develop. What an exciting adventure to realize that the Holy Spirit can work within and through a person to accomplish the will of the sovereign God!

Lori taught me about loving unconditionally, which, from my perspective, is at the core of all caregiving, all social justice, and all of the very best efforts at evangelism and Christian discipleship.

So let me share with you my path for a few pages. Perhaps you will see yourself in different applications leading to similar conclusions.

Booker T. and an Opportunity for Relating to Others "Not Like Me"

My journey toward becoming a caregiver began with a concern more for justice, perhaps, than true need-meeting.

I was a high school student in the early 1970s, in a part of the world that was largely segregated racially. During my growing-up years, I lived in a white part of town and had white friends. I did not, however, grow up in a home that openly espoused white supremacy; I didn't grow up hearing the adults around me advocate segregation or voice racist comments. The separation of black and white in my world was simply that—a separation that I didn't think much about.

I was too young to understand much about the race riot that rocked Tulsa in an earlier decade and destroyed many of the businesses and buildings in the black neighborhoods. I knew there had been "trouble," but I also knew that my parents and immediate circle of friends had not participated in it or been affected by it to any great degree. One might say I was racially naïve.

Then government mandates for integration began. The terms *busing* and *quotas* began to enter the cultural conversation.

Tulsa had an outstanding all-black school, Booker T. Washington High School, known by most simply as *Booker T*. The school had excelled in athletics but also was well known across the state of Oklahoma as a school with high academic standards and cultural events (music and theater). Booker T. was admired by many white educators and citizens, although not "desired" necessarily as a place where white families wanted their children to attend.

One of the readily observed factors about Booker T. was that it truly was the hub of the black community—like a large diamond in a gold setting. The black community life revolved around the school schedule and school events. The school was even more revered than most of the black churches in the north Tulsa neighborhoods. Everybody in the black community seemed to know what was happening at Booker T., which was succeeding in whatever area of endeavor was mentioned and whose leaders were the school administration, coaching staff, and faculty.

The pride factor related to being a student at Booker T. Washington High School was very high in the black neighborhoods of Tulsa. Perhaps for this reason above others, the administrators at Booker T. did not like the government-set standards for integration, and they chose to walk a different path.

Rather than adopt a procedure for implementing the mandated integration regulations according to numerical statistics and neighborhood bus routes, Booker T. administrators said, in essence, "We are going to create such an outstanding and diverse curriculum, with such high standards, that white students will *want* to attend Booker T. Those who want to attend will be welcomed, and the Tulsa Public School system will provide transportation to the school."

The new Booker T. curriculum was broad and enticing. A number of foreign languages were offered, most of which were not available at any other school in the state (language classes included Russian and Mandarin). The new teaching staff had excellent credentials, and the school administrators made it clear that the teachers at Booker T. were going to demand truly outstanding academic performance.

I wanted to be a part of that. I told my parents that I had every intention of applying for and attending Booker T. Washington. I'm not sure they were entirely pleased with my choice, but they didn't keep me from pursuing the application process, and after I was accepted, they didn't keep me from attending Booker T.

I was excited about the curriculum I would be facing. I was excited about the opportunity to mingle with students who were not "just like me." And perhaps most of all, I had already developed a sense of justice that made me want to be part of a groundbreaking racial integration effort that was innovative and enviable. I was all for integration and all for equality of the races, but I was also eager to see things in my life proceed in an orderly, excellent, and not particularly radical way. In other words, I was a radical in theory, but not necessarily a radical who would have pursued protest rallies or violence. My rebellion against the status quo was going to Booker T.

I'm glad I did. Not only was the experience outstanding in all regards, but it set me on a path of realizing that there are many ways to seek justice for social ills and to defend and pursue socially worthy causes. I learned through experience at Booker T. that peaceful and innovative methods are often far more productive and lasting than disruptive, headline-seeking methods.

At Booker T., I worked on the yearbook staff, which gave me tremendous insight into the social organization of the black community and allowed me a window into the worlds of some of the brightest and most talented people I have ever known—both teachers and students. A major lesson for me was this: poverty and race do not *necessarily* define a person. They may be factors in a person's identity, but excellence in performance can rise above socioeconomic status and race.

At this point, I should perhaps point out that I am part Cherokee. Like many people in Oklahoma, I don't have to look far to find a "full blood" in my family tree. However, I did not grow up speaking Cherokee or participating in many of the Cherokee cultural events. Because American Indian heritage is so prominent in Oklahoma, I never felt any sting of prejudice related to race. Even so, having American Indian blood may also have been a factor in my quickness to embrace racial diversity and to seek out and applaud excellence wherever I found it, male or female … black, white, or American Indian … poor or not poor.

Jesus Christ—A Reason for Everything Else in Life

As a young child, I was baptized in the United Methodist Church, and in many ways, I have been connected to the Methodist Church my entire life.

When I was nine years old, my family moved from Muskogee, Oklahoma, to Tulsa. Our next-door neighbors were the Smith family—C.R. and Hazel, and their three children, Kevin, Karen, and Kelly. The Smith family invited my family to go to church with them at Will Rogers United Methodist Church. In retrospect, it seems amazing to me that my Methodist family moved next door to another Methodist family. Kelly Smith became Kelly Junk, now our Director of Global Outreach at First United Methodist Church.

At Will Rogers Methodist Church I attended Vacation Bible School and Sunday school, sang in choirs, participated in the youth group, and even went on mission trips. Hazel Smith was a spiritual mentor for me until I graduated from high school.

Will Rogers United Methodist Church hosted a lay witness mission when I was thirteen years old. It was during that weekend that I truly made a personal commitment to Jesus Christ, accepting Him as my Savior and making Him the Lord of my life. I have never wavered from that commitment I made at age thirteen. It was the start of an exciting journey for me, and as the years went by, my passion increased for the Lord and for serving Him in whatever way He might direct. Even though I am quiet by nature, I couldn't seem to help but tell people about the Lord wherever I went. I often handed out tracts to those I met at the 7-Eleven convenience store, even to the cashier!

After I finished my undergraduate degree in nursing (1980), I went to Costa Rica on a missions adventure. God sightings were everywhere. My love for the Lord increased greatly, and I was more committed than ever to finding as many ways as possible to serve the Lord.

I later spent a year (1985–1986) in Aberdeen, Scotland, working for an international ministry called Teen Challenge. I had been on a number of mission trips by that time, but this was my first experience actually living for an extended period in another nation, away from family and friends. Even though the language of Scotland is English, I felt very much a foreigner in a foreign land. I learned new vocabulary words and new ways of relating to others around me. I also learned new ways about how to rely on God in areas of my life where I previously thought I could be self-sufficient. It was not the easiest time in my life, but it certainly was one of my most life-changing growth experiences.

In 1986, I began a Master of Arts degree in counseling at Oral Roberts University in Tulsa.

Lori—A "Wounded Traveler" God Put in My Path

Lori Rickman was twenty-three years old when I first met her. She had come to Tulsa after meeting John Jacobs and his Power Team, which she had first seen in California (the Power Team was a group of strongmen who very effectively used their athletic strength to witness to young people). John and his team had told Lori that if she was willing to turn her life around, they would provide the financial means for her to go to the City of Faith Medical Center in Tulsa for rehab.

The year was 1987. I was attending Oral Roberts University, across the street to the north of the City of Faith Medical Center. I had completed an undergraduate degree in nursing and was working as a nurse in a chemical dependency unit of the City of Faith Hospital.

It was the night shift, and I went into the "new admits" room to set up the routine lab work required. I introduced myself to the young woman there. As I drew her blood, she said, "I love needles." She was sincere! She meant her statement for shock effect, and it worked. Lori was the only person I've ever met, by the way, who looked cute in a mohawk haircut.

From that first encounter, I quickly learned that Lori was a person who could always be counted on to press others for honesty and transparency. Although she was guarded, she delivered it personally and required it of others.

After Lori was released from the hospital, having completed the chemical dependency protocol, she needed a place to live, and several of us banded together to get her an apartment. Living on her own didn't work for Lori, however, and a few weeks later she came to live with me—and stayed with me for seven years.

Lori was the catalyst for my meeting many people I would not otherwise have met, and for my facing many issues and questions I may never have addressed. Some of the people I met were instrumental in my eventually seeking to become ordained and to pursuing and earning a Doctor of Ministry degree. I believe, the person doing the ministry tends to learn, grow, and change as much *or more* than those who are receiving the person's caregiving. That certainly was the case in my relationship with Lori. The main lessons God taught me in my relationship with her were lessons of God's grace and unconditional love.

James 1:2–4 became a hallmark passage of the Bible for me: "Count it all joy when you fall into various trials, knowing that the testing of your faith produces patience. But let patience have its perfect work, that you may be perfect and complete, lacking nothing." There were many times when sheer perseverance—the manifestation of patience—was the soil in which I had to root my attitude. Lori challenged me, wore me out, stretched me, and loved me.

Lori knew all the lyrics and artists involved in Christian music during the late 1980s. She loved cats, liked to eat out, and loved to shop. I didn't enjoy or appreciate any of those three when I first met Lori, but *I* came to love cats, dining out, and shopping—and to enjoy watching how much *she* enjoyed those things. Perhaps more than any person I have ever known, Lori embodied the old quote, "Sing like no one is listening. Love like you've never been hurt. Dance like no one is watching."

I don't know what kind of relationship the Good Samaritan might have developed with the wounded traveler he helped—perhaps that is in a longer version of a story that Jesus will one day tell us in eternity—but I do know that all caregiving boils down to the highest and lowest points of our learning to love just one person in need. When we truly love a person with God's unconditional love, we discover that the person *can* change, and so can we.

> When we can truly love a person with God's unconditional love, we discover that the person *can* change, and so can we.

In December 2013, I was stunned when I received the call that Lori had died. She had just turned 49 three weeks before. She had struggled with multiple sclerosis for a number of years, but she had retained her sparkling smile and unusual sense of style in spite of her physical limitations. Before the MS robbed her fingers of dexterity, she created artistic masterpieces—from cards to jewelry to calligraphy. She loved texture and color.

There was nothing about MS that kept Lori from being intuitive. She could read people from a mile away. She was also exceedingly persistent. She refused to allow pain to control the whole of her life or to rob her of good times with others. She was a living example to me that a person can be mature, content, peaceful, giving, loving, and thankful even in the "worst" of times and conditions.

Lori taught me how to see the potential for love and faith in every person—specifically, to see the potential of *any* human life from *God's* perspective. Lori taught me how to see every person I encounter as a recipient of God's grace, love, and forgiveness—and to see every person as a challenge to me to display God's grace, love, and forgiveness to them.

And What Does This Have to Do with *You*?

I hope my story can be a catalyst for you to ask yourself three questions that lie at the core of a true caregiving spirit:

- Do you want to make a difference in your world for good?
- Do you want to follow Jesus Christ as closely as you can, no matter where He might lead you?
- Do you know what it means to love unconditionally?

If your answer is even a partial *yes* to these questions, let me assure you with boldness: You are qualified to be in a caregiving ministry! This just may be God's call to you to sign on to a ministry you have been considering!

If your answer is *no* to any of these, I encourage you to engage in some personal introspection and prayer. My admonition to you is this: God has something *more* for you. If you will avail yourself of *His* leading and help, that something more will be *good*, both good for you and good for others.

4

Our Beginnings in
Community Ministries

No ministry program emerges out of a vacuum—God always identifies
a field to sow and needs to address *prior* to the start of an official outreach of
ministry.

It's also true that no ministry program emerges without God having already
prepared a "champion" for the outreach or ministry He has in mind. Note that
I did not use the word *leader.* A champion is a person who speaks out clearly
and courageously about a need, or who advocates that a ministry be developed
to address a need. The person may not become the organizational leader for the
ministry in the ensuing months or years, although a champion certainly can be
the leader.

I'm absolutely convinced of the truth of those two statements. Not only does
the Bible present these concepts, but I've seen more examples than I can begin to
recount.

The Good Samaritan in the story Jesus told may have been a real person
Jesus knew or about whom Jesus had heard. He may have been a composite
character developed by Jesus to convey His message. Either way, this Good
Samaritan has become a champion for caregiving for more than two thousand
years. His actions inspire and convict. Many of us in caregiving and volunteer
ministry roles today look to the Good Samaritan as the Bible "hero" that the
Holy Spirit used to convict us about a need or to compel us to take action to seek
justice on behalf of another person or healing for our fellow life-travelers who
are wounded or in need.

Every volunteer ministry with which I have been involved, and especially so
in the last twenty years, has had one or more "champions," some of whom at the
outset of a ministry and others taking a champion turn as a ministry's baton is
passed from advocate to advocate through the years and from project to project.

James Buskirk—Originator and Champion for Community Ministries

To those who have been members at First United Methodist Church for many years, it seems as if the church has always been reaching out to the Tulsa community. However, that was not always the case.

When Dr. James Buskirk came to First Methodist as senior minister in 1984, the church was involved in two local outreaches—Meals on Wheels and Destination Discovery. It was a time when Tulsa's economy was in trouble and many people were hungry and in need. Dr. Buskirk brought a vision for church members to minister to persons outside the walls of the church and boldly proclaimed this was a ministry and direction whose "time was obvious." In his first year at the church, "Dr. B" (as he has been called affectionately by many members) started community ministries through a Motivation for Ministry weekend. He believed in evangelism through lay service to help lay people be who they were created to be.

Dr. Buskirk's passion to see laity evangelize through serving began while working on his doctorate at Candler School of Theology at Emory University. Prior to becoming the senior minister at First United Methodist, Dr. Buskirk had done his doctoral dissertation in the area of community ministry at Candler, where he was the originator and forerunner of Motivation for Ministry. This multi-day training program challenges believers to recognize needs in their community and then exercise "holy want-to" to meet those needs. Dr. Buskirk had been invited to conduct a number of these lay ministry training sessions at churches across the South, and the Motivation for Ministry model became the cornerstone of our new community ministries emphasis at First United Methodist.

The Motivation for Ministry Process

The process begins by asking people two questions:

1. What needs do you see in this community to which you *wish* this church might respond?

2. To which of these needs do *you* feel *called*?

    As First United Methodist embarked on asking and answering these questions, church members began to see *as a church body* that the needs and the people with the skills and desire to address those needs were linked. There was little need to strong-arm anyone into ministry.

The Motivation for Ministry process also asks this third question:

3. Where do you see an opportunity for ministry that others in the church might do with you?

These program presentations also give information about *how* people might work together to respond to needs in various communities adjacent to, or close to, the church. The program includes a system for serving through "ministry groups," essentially teams of people working together.

During the Motivation for Ministry two-day event, the leaders passed out a survey to get written responses as feedback. After the first and largest Motivation for Ministry weekend, First United Methodist had 1,600 suggestions for ministry!

The suggestions were divided into various ministry categories—in all, forty-nine categories. A meeting place within the church was assigned to each of those categories. Participants were then invited to go to the room of the category of ministry that interested them the most. If there were fewer than four people in the room, they were asked to move to another room and another category.

At the end of the weekend, First Methodist had thirty-nine ministry groups with at least four people—one group had sixty people! The leaders then asked people to meet with their group before they made a decision to continue. After six weeks, the church had twenty-nine strong new ministries with about three hundred people willing to commit to their chosen ministry for at least six months.

Some of the ministries were professional, such as a dental clinic and a legal counseling ministry.

Some groups wanted to pursue ministry to specific groups of people, such as unwed mothers, students who needed tutoring, people who needed help with odd jobs and home repairs, and even people who needed a reliable used car.

One group wanted to engage in a ministry for the deaf, and another wanted to establish a furniture-moving ministry for those unable to move their belongings (they called themselves "Moving in the Spirit"). There was a ministry to the elderly that dubbed itself "Young at Heart."

After six months, another meeting was held as an opportunity for those involved to "reset" their ministry goals. Most of those involved did not want to quit their ministry, but a few felt the need to alter their ministry or add a new dimension to it. We thought it was important to give volunteers the opportunity to take a break if they felt it was the season of their life to do so. People shouldn't have to die to get out of a ministry.

The church leadership learned a great lesson: there were people in our midst who *wanted* to be active in helping but who had not been given an opportunity to provide help. These people simply needed to be invited to become part of a servant-heart ministry and to be given an opportunity to put their own creative stamp on it.

Jessica Moffatt—Also a Champion

The first year after he assumed the senior minister role, Dr. Buskirk hired Reverend Jessica Moffatt to serve as minister of community ministries, which she did from 1985 to 1994. I cannot imagine a more enthusiastic or effective champion for recruiting the laity into heartfelt and effective volunteer ministry.

Jessica asked in a sermon one Sunday, "What position, possession, passion, or preparation do you have that can be used for ministry?" She wasn't expecting someone to say, "I have a Learjet," but someone went to her with a willingness to use his jet for ministry. The next Sunday she asked, "Someone said he has a jet. So all of you who have airplanes, call me."

They did. And within two weeks, six or seven pilots in the church had banded together, calling themselves "Christ's Air Cavalry".

Not long after that, a terrible accident occurred in the greater Tulsa community: everyone in a family died except for one young woman who needed to get to family members who could care for her in New York. Jessica had every good intention of calling one of the pilots in the new "Cavalry," but before she could make the call, one of these pilots had heard about the need on the news and had called to volunteer.

That one example inspired many in the church to become very *proactive* in finding ways to identify neighbors we could help with *unused resources or skills we were willing to put into ministry service.* The Holy Spirit seemed to nudge various people in our congregation to do what they did best or enjoyed most into a form of active service to people in need. It was a groundswell movement that God Himself orchestrated!

Through the years, the members of First United Methodist have grown accustomed to hearing, "We in community ministries want to hear *your* dreams and to facilitate the difference that your dreams, your talents, and your passions can have on other people in the name of Christ." The church regards *every* member as the opening chapter for a new ministry of some type.

God can use every person who is willing to be used! Nothing is insignificant when it is placed in His hands and subjected to His leadership.

On the Shoulders of Giants

As I mentioned earlier, I worked in Scotland for a year as part of a ministry devoted to transforming communities with the gospel. While I saw good fruit in the evangelistic ministry done there, I didn't see a lot of evidence that the evangelism had translated into true community transformation. That isn't to say that it didn't happen—either then or later—but I didn't see it.

I came home in 1986 with a strong desire to see a community genuinely transformed by a group of Christians serving the Lord. In 1994, Dr. Buskirk hired me to be the next minister of community ministries. By nature, I am a behind-the-scenes person, and I counted it a high privilege to work alongside Jessica Moffatt.

Jessica is a very charismatic and gifted communicator. I learned a great deal from her, but I was also aware that we were very different and that God would use me in ways that were decidedly within the parameters of my personality and abilities. It was an important lesson to learn that I did not need to be "just like" Jessica in order to do what God was asking me to do. I just needed to be the best Connie I could be.

I share that for this reason: those who work in volunteer positions nearly always receive the baton of leadership from someone before them, perhaps someone who has been there for a considerable length of time and who has established a reputation for success. In turn, they will one day pass the baton of leadership on to the next person.

It is vitally important that each person along the track of the relay race understand that God uses people of all types of personality, in a wide variety of ways, at certain seasons of life (both their life and the life of the ministry) and for certain purposes. We are each called to find God's plan and purpose for *our* service. What is essential is that we desire to have a servant's heart, desire to hear from the Holy Spirit in an ongoing way, and desire to do the work the Lord sets before us with love, compassion, faith, and perseverance.

We *need* each other.

Volunteers need fellow volunteers—their ideas, their friendship, their wise counsel, and, at times, their applause or their shoulders to cry on.

Volunteers must also be aware that those who are served need them—in ways they may not know and in ways that may not ever be revealed fully. Nevertheless, volunteers must assume that solely because the Lord has divinely connected them to certain individuals in need, He has a plan for their relationship with that person to yield a measure of His grace, mercy, forgiveness, and love. Their need and God's plan for them to be a purveyor of His presence are all that is required to have a purpose in ministry.

Shortly after Dr. B asked me to be the minister of community ministries in 1994, he challenged me to look for something else we could do in the community that was different from what we were already doing in community ministries.

With that purpose in mind, I attended a men's breakfast. I readily admit I did not fully realize at the time that this was intended to be a breakfast to which only men were invited. I was made to feel welcome, nonetheless, and at this breakfast, I talked with Dr. John Thompson, the Tulsa school superintendent, who was the guest speaker. I asked him what a church might do for or with the school system.

He replied, "Why don't you adopt a school?"

It was a simple question, but it led to a profound answer.

The word *adopt* became a critical concept in our decision-making. Dr. Thompson had not invited us to "get involved with" or "volunteer at" or "work alongside" or "participate with." He used the word adopt, and adoption in both the Bible and in the legal system of our day is a *permanent relationship*. There is no "adopting" for a month or two or even a year or two. Adoption is a lasting commitment.

We began to explore what it might mean to adopt a school even before we located a school to adopt. It took us months of meeting, discussing, and praying about adopting a school before we made a practical, tangible move in that direction. I am grateful for the "think time" that went into the decision. We went into adopting a school with our eyes wide open and a very deep sense of responsibility that if we started down this path, we were in it for the long haul, *no matter what.*

Meanwhile …

As I mentioned, God calls people to a ministry that *He* has already designated. That certainly was a truth we encountered in a very obvious and direct way.

In 1983, the Tulsa Metropolitan Chamber established an "Adopt A School" program, which today is called "Partners in Education," to link community resources and Tulsa's school-age children. The program provided a foundation for our growing desire to adopt a school.

In 1995, David Moncrief, a member of First United Methodist, introduced me to Don and Emily Renberg. They frequently attended First Methodist but were not members of the church. The Renbergs had already established relationships with administrators, staff, and students at the nearby Eugene Field Elementary School.

It was a good day when I met Emily and Don! They were immediately my Christian sister and brother. They had come to First United Methodist to tell one of our Sunday school classes about volunteer opportunities at Eugene Field. They spoke about their work there and then humbly and simply asked if there was anybody at our church who might want to become involved with them.

A group of interested members and I met with the Renbergs in the Eugene Field library. We sat in the tiny library chairs used by the children as we were introduced to the school by Principal Betty McIlvain, various Eugene Field students, and the Tulsa school district's volunteer coordinator, Reba Luton. It was a "birthing" time for a tremendous outreach, although most of the people in the room could not foresee the scope or impact of what lay ahead. Even so, it was an exciting day.

Emily had been volunteering at the school as something of a teacher's aide-at-large. She had an amazing spiritual gift of discernment and could quickly and accurately assess the needs of an individual student and then see how to meet those needs. She was a teacher by training, as was her mother, Caroline Rose, who also volunteered with her. Don was brought into the volunteer arena in a big way one summer when a serious staffing need arose. He was a big hit with the children, and they quickly won his heart.

Together, the Renbergs had been the leaders of a summer school program at Eugene Field for two years before they introduced First United Methodist to the school.

I think it is valuable to note that neither Emily nor her mother, Caroline, were looking for "jobs," but rather for an opportunity to add purpose and significance to their lives. They had a deep love for children and a desire to be of service, and perhaps most of all, the perseverance and patience to outlast any problem they encountered. Both of them, and Don as well, took the time and gave the attention necessary to develop a true *personal* relationship with every child at the school. For many of the children, Emily, Caroline, and Don were the first non-family, non-teacher adults who knew them by name and were steady in their concern for their whole life, not just their academic life. They were a family on a *mission* to make a difference in the name of Jesus. Emily, Caroline, and Don each believed strongly that the cycle of poverty in the lives of Eugene Field students could be broken if a sufficient number of caring adults invested their time and love. They pursued that belief with nonstop effort!

We at First United Methodist were impressed with the depth of their commitment and the quality of their faith. Their pioneer work at the school made our decision to adopt a school easy—and the choice of Eugene Field Elementary School became obvious.

In May 1995, First United Methodist Church officially adopted Eugene Field Elementary School through the Tulsa Public Schools program.

Other Programs Also Began to Take Root

Our adoption of Eugene Field Elementary was not the only community-ministry outreach established in the 1990s. As just one example, a church member took a church-sponsored class called "Network," which focused on identifying members' passion, personal style, and spiritual gifts. She concluded, "I love to go to garage sales and hold garage sales." I suggested to her, "Why don't you do a garage sale ministry?"

She wasn't sure going to garage sales was a ministry, but two years later, she came to me and said, "I'm ready to do it." She and a group of her friends became the garage sale ministry that gave members of First United Methodist the opportunity to donate their gently used and new items in exchange for a donation receipt. From the mountain of items donated, she and her team put together a large number of kits for Tulsa's Day Center for the Homeless, especially kits designed to help homeless individuals and families as they moved out of the city shelter and into more permanent accommodations.

In the 1980s and 1990s, a number of other outreach ministries were also planted and took root. Some continue to flourish in our midst:

- Flower Ministry
- Car Ministry
- Prison Ministry
- Job Ministry (now called Overcoming Job Transition)
- Prayer Card Ministry
- WWJD and Soup for the Soul Ministries to the Homeless
- Restore Hope (community ministries volunteers assist this established agency, which is an affiliate of the Oklahoma Conference of the United Methodist church)

In addition, a variety of ministries have been established through our involvement with Eugene Field Elementary that are more recent.

5

Eugene Field Elementary School—
Our Wounded Traveler

In the terms of the Good Samaritan parable told by Jesus, Eugene Field Elementary School became our "wounded traveler."

In seeking to "bind up the wounds," we truly discovered just how wounded the students were at this troubled school.

We did our homework when it came to learning about the students and their families. Here are four key facts we documented and shared with our volunteers:

- There are five major ethnic groups at Eugene Field: Caucasian, Hispanic, African American, Asian, and American Indian.

- Ninety-seven percent of the children are on the government-sponsored meal program, receiving free lunches and breakfasts.

- A significant percentage of the students come from very difficult home environments. Many of the students come from single-parent homes, most often fatherless.

- Eugene Field Elementary School is considered to be one of the schools with the highest rate of family poverty, if not the highest, in the entire Tulsa elementary school system.

We knew we had serious "healing" work to do!

Initially, we envisioned three distinct ways our members at First United Methodist might be involved—first, as "friends" (who might give practical and educational assistance); second, as classroom assistants of some type; and third, as sponsors, adult chaperones, or adult participants for an existing school club or school field trip.

All three of those functions took off immediately and remain in some form today, twenty years later.

First Friends Become Lunch Buddies and Mentors

As we at First United Methodist Church became involved with the school, Emily and Don headed up a program we called "First Friends." I was privileged to work with them on this initiative. We had no difficulty in recruiting volunteers, and soon, we had on any given day as many as ninety people going from First United Methodist Church to mentor the children. These "First Friends" usually went to the school once a week, although many went more than once a week.

Our initial goal was to see each child matched with a mentor who would eat lunch with the child one day a week, play games and read with the child, and, over time, build a good relationship that could yield communication about a wide variety of life issues.

The main academic activity for mentoring was reading, but a number of our mentors through the years have also helped their mentees with English, spelling, and math. Beyond a reading time, mentors simply listened to the children, answered their questions, and became role models in their lives.

Mentors are often assigned by schools to students who are doing poorly or behaving badly. That was not the approach taken by Eugene Field's principal. At Eugene Field, mentors were assigned to students who showed academic potential and who were behaving well.

It quickly became a privilege at Eugene Field for a student to be given a mentor—having a mentor became an "honor," and the students began to *desire* mentors more and more.

Emily took personal responsibility for helping match up our First United Methodist volunteers with children. She knew the children well enough to know which personalities might click with the volunteers who were becoming their friends.

Every mentor underwent a background check. As much as possible, men were assigned to boys and women were placed with girls. Every volunteer was evaluated for his or her caring heart and genuine appreciation for children.

The mentors agreed to spend at least thirty minutes a week with the student to whom they were assigned. That may not seem like a lot of time, but thirty minutes a week of one-on-one time with a caring adult was very often thirty more minutes than a child received from all other non-school-related adults combined! Dr. Betty McIlvain, the first principal we served alongside, even allowed First Friends to call or email their Eugene Field mentees during school hours.

Mentor volunteers usually brought lunch for their friend to the school. The hallways would be filled with First Friends and children meeting to eat lunch together. After-lunch activities included playing games with the students or working on reading or math worksheets.

Emily put together a volunteer resources room that she filled with grade-appropriate books and activities. At times, a mentor might read a few paragraphs, but in most cases, the mentor listened intently as the *child* read. Often, the circumstances of extreme poverty can mean that children get little adult attention at home from a parent or parents who are overwhelmed and overworked. Unless you have been a mentor in a situation like this, you may not realize just how valuable it is to a child to be the center of attention, having a kind and caring adult hang on your every word.

The Big Bucks Store

One of the most innovative programs that we began in our first year of volunteering at Eugene Field was the "Big Bucks Store." The store allowed students from first through fifth grades to earn "big bucks" (play money) for excellent behavior, perfect attendance, completed homework, and service projects. The children were then given the privilege of spending their big bucks to purchase quality items from the Big Bucks Store. In many cases, the students spent their big bucks on gifts for family members and friends.

Church members who worked in the fashion industry used their skills to set up a fashion show to kick off the Big Bucks Store. Children from the school were quick to volunteer as models. It was a big hit.

Gathering the Merchandise. In the beginning days of the store, calls went out periodically to the whole church for donations of new and almost-new toys, books, games, and toiletry items.

Members of First United Methodist took these donations of both new and gently used items from parishioners, as well as items from some retail outlets that regarded the Big Bucks Store as a means of charitable service to the needy, and organized the items in various categories.

At First United Methodist, we set up a large Big Bucks Box under a staircase, and even now, rarely a week goes by without a generous number of items being donated.

In the beginning, new items included batteries, deodorant, toothpaste, laundry soap, dryer sheets, dishwashing liquid, and school supplies.

Gently used items included toys, sports equipment, board games, and sports clothing (often linked to the University of Oklahoma or Oklahoma State University). Items have also included a wide assortment of age-appropriate books, jewelry, and art supplies.

The children, especially girls, seem drawn toward jewelry, bath and body items, and gifts for family members. The boys gravitate toward games and sports equipment and gifts for their moms. Gift bags are also made available and are a favorite item when children are shopping for family members and friends.

Volunteers from the church staff the Big Bucks Store, and some of them have found the experience so personally rewarding that they have volunteered in the store for years, developing ongoing relationships with the children that are marked by love and faithfulness.

The adult interaction in the store is often directed toward helping students make wise buying decisions, teaching the children how to handle merchandise respectfully, and encouraging children to enjoy delayed gratification. They have even introduced the children to the retail concept of lay-away!

Volunteers are also shoppers for the store when money donations are given for the store—they tend to get more bang for the buck by shopping at garage sales and big-lot stores.

Logistics Related to the Store's Operation. Today, the Big Bucks Store is open on Friday mornings and closed during school vacation times.

Students can earn up to four Big Bucks in each "shopping period" (generally every one to two weeks, depending on the school schedule).

The store is housed in a trailer—there is one room for items costing one to two Big Bucks and another room with items costing three or more.

A major goal for the store is to help children feel empowered by the opportunity to make buying choices—something many of them have never experienced before—and to help them make *good* choices that they don't regret later. The adult volunteers model and encourage kindness. They also wrap the gifts children choose for a parent.

There are frequent discussions about "why" a student may not have earned as many Big Bucks as desired—most of the children readily understand and acknowledge that they had too many absences from school or didn't do all of their homework on time. They also come to understand why they can't buy a three- or four-dollar item with only two Big Bucks.

The layaway room has items that children select that are higher priced. It sometimes takes two or three months for a child to earn enough Big Bucks to get his or her item out of layaway.

Lessons Learned in the Shopping. The store is not primarily about children "getting stuff," although the things given and "purchased" are greatly desired and appreciated by children in poverty. The message is also about financial responsibility and teaching children to be patient and to persevere in their pursuit of goals.

A former Big Bucks coordinator, Sharon McMahon, had this to say about the store: "I have watched a whole set of kids grow up and come through the store—from early childhood to fifth grade. I've watched them go from barely recognizing their numbers to being creative in figuring out how to buy an item. One time in particular, there was a boxed set of nineteen craft pens and three little girls. The 'lobbyist' for the trio approached me and asked if by putting their Big Bucks together, they might buy the set. Among themselves, they had *exactly* the amount needed to buy the set. They purchased the set together, but then faced the challenge of dividing nineteen pens among three purchasers. I suggested they give an extra pen to the 'lobbyist' as a bonus for her effort. They agreed. It was a great life lesson!"

Sharon also told of students who saved a long time for a particular item … of students who chose to purchase notebook paper instead of toys to help a family's budget … and students who banded together to help replace a fellow student's purchase that had been damaged. Sharon once said, "I saw one little boy truly learn *not* to steal."

The Big Bucks Store developed an International Corner, which has featured items made in Egypt, Russia, Bolivia, England, and other nations. The items have made geography and history come alive for more than one student.

Overall, the children treat the store with a great deal of respect—they know it is *their* store—and they can often be heard encouraging one another to "earn more" and "spend on gifts."

Debi Emery and Jill Miller are the present Big Bucks Store champions. They have taken the store to another level. The Big Bucks Store looks like a specialty gift store. There is a section for teachers and staff along with a coffee machine. The customer service is amazing. Every holiday is a special occasion in the store.

The Bicycle Club Has Been a Popular Activity for 20 Years!

The Eugene Field Bicycle Club has been a very popular program involving First United Methodist volunteers. Dick Banks, an avid cyclist and church member, along with two Eugene Field Elementary School teachers who commuted on bicycles, started the club in 1996.

Students apply for and are accepted into the Bicycle Club based on a desire to participate and a recommendation from their teachers. By drawing, they select a bike that has been refurbished by volunteers at First Methodist. They are taught bicycle safety and how to ride both on streets and on the trail.

On the first day, they select and adjust the bikes and helmets and take a short ride on River Parks Trail along the Arkansas River. The rides get longer each day, and the last ride can be more than ten miles. If riders complete the increasingly difficult rides, they earn and get to keep their scholarship bike, a helmet, a lock, and a cool Bicycle Club T-shirt. More importantly, they are praised for their accomplishment.

In May 2016, Dick Banks retired from the Eugene Field Bicycle Club. At age 85, he is still young at heart and continues in ministry providing refurbished bicycles to the poor and homeless for much needed transportation.

Birthday Parties

Volunteers and school administrators quickly gravitated toward the idea of holding birthday celebrations for the children. For many years, Gayla Dixon was the birthday party champion. Gayla and her team, including her husband Richard, truly made the children feel celebrated at each birthday party. Initially, these parties were held monthly at our Youth and Family Center, and later, once a quarter. In the fall of 2015, we began celebrating birthdays at our monthly community dinners.

We did a tally in 2015 and found that more than ninety-five Eugene Field birthday parties have been hosted by volunteers from First United Methodist since the mid-1990s.

Clean-Up and Playground Improvement Efforts

Community outreach continued to expand when Dr. Wade Paschal became senior minister at First Methodist in 2001. All-day, all-church workdays were organized and Dr. Paschal rolled up his sleeves working alongside the hundreds of congregants in work teams as "fully committed followers of Christ." Volunteers turned out with weed-eaters, paint brushes, hammers, and ladders to spruce up fences and yards and make home repairs and renovations around the city and across the bridge in the Eugene Field area.

Throughout the year, volunteers from the Eugene Field neighborhood and the church worked together on clean-up days at the school, helping with landscaping and general maintenance. Volunteers also sponsored playground equipment and benches, and some assisted in the painting of decorative murals at the school. Diversity of service has flourished.

Prayer Walks and Special Events

Especially in the early years, volunteers often went on simple prayer walks around and through the school building. In the beginning, teachers and staff were treated to FUMC's Christmastime Madrigal dinners. First United

Methodist volunteers co-hosted Attendance Awards Lunches for children, with staff members serving, providing decorations, and assisting in planning the event.

Some of these events and activities were short-lived—lasting perhaps only a year or two. Some of the events were co-sponsored with other groups such as West Tulsa United Methodist Church, Phoenix Avenue Baptist Church, Salvation Army, Good Samaritan Health Clinic, and the Tulsa Housing Authority. Other events have been ongoing for more than twenty years!

The length of operation time should not be equated to the impact of an outreach ministry. At times, an outreach may have had a tremendous impact but was perhaps directed toward the meeting of a specific need or was reflective of a particular volunteer's skills. Like most things in creation, volunteer efforts tend to have a season—they are planted, grow, and yield a harvest that may be annual or perpetual.

We have always been quick to look for opportunities, especially those opportunities that seemed to be God inspired—for example, if a wholesaler gave us a large quantity of excess merchandise, we never turned down the gift because it didn't fit a specific program. Rather, we tended to develop a new program to use the gift. In doing this, we were careful never to assume that the wholesaler would return the next year with a donation of any size or type. If that happened, great! If it didn't happen, we didn't mourn the loss of something not given, but rather received and rejoiced at those things the Lord put into our hands.

In a few cases, at their own initiative, Sunday school classes at First United Methodist collected funds aimed at special projects. For example, the money collected at the 2002 Christmas party held by the Beacon Class went exclusively for the birthday party held in January 2003. The Builders Sunday school class collects money for the school library. The Carpenters Sunday school class has sponsored community dinners and birthday parties. The Patria and One in the Spirit classes have sponsored camp registrations.

Where the School Led, We Followed

Through the years, we have with worked four principals at Eugene Field: Dr. Betty McIlvain, (1990 to 1999), Betty Bell Clapp (1999 to 2003), Cindi Hemm (2003 to 2012), and Dr. Sheila Riley (2012 to present).

Each woman brought distinctive strengths and personal style—and faith—to her role as principal.

At the outset of every school year, I have made it a priority to meet with the principal, and I have taken laity with me whenever possible. Over the years, we discerned that the church was functioning as a bridge from one principal to the next—we were a constant that had not existed in this community before.

I met with each principal to offer our support and prayers and to ask how we might help. First United Methodist's desire since 1995 has been to invest in the school's vision and to support the school.

Betty McIlvain was the first principal with whom we worked. She became a great advocate within the school community as a whole for having a church group *serve* a school. She was always open to our ideas about ways in which we might serve the school. She was a strong leader who set very clear parameters for her teachers, staff members, and us as volunteers. Dr. McIlvain's openness to First Methodist's involvement, her support of the church and our volunteers, and her willingness to go the extra mile to welcome us and help us serve established the strong foundation that our outreach to Eugene Field is built upon today.

We came to realize early on, however, that our work as volunteers from First United Methodist was regarded as something of a constant at the school. We were not opposed to administrative changes, and we quickly found ways to adapt to various leadership styles and embrace new administrative goals. At the same time, the teachers, support staff members, parents, and, most importantly, the children came to see their mentors and the volunteers from First United Methodist as a unifying thread of love and care.

Betty McIlvain was followed in the principal role by Betty Bell Clapp, who gave support to all of the programs we had going at the school and who was also a powerful prayer warrior for the school, its children, and the teachers, as well as the volunteers and parents.

The next principal was Cindi Hemm, who was a great activist and visionary. When we asked, "How might we help you?" she replied in very practical terms that the school needed five things: clothes for the children, food for the children, funds to help with school supplies and equipment, love, and prayers for the community as a whole.

We were happy to provide what we could without hesitation! We knew we had members who would give abundant love as well as fervent prayer. We believed that we would be able to acquire and provide clothing and food without any bureaucratic complications or conditions. We weren't sure how much money we might be able to raise, so we could make no commitment at that time about dollar amounts, but we also expressed optimism that we could raise some money, or else gifts in kind to help with supplies and equipment, and later, help for some of the children to go to summer camps. Cindi is passionate about children. She is a gifted storyteller and continues to tell her Eugene Field story today.[1]

Cindi was followed by Sheila Riley, the current principal. She is especially strong on accountability and responsibility. Her innovations involve the teachers and staff as well as the children and, in turn, us as volunteers. Dr. Riley's life experiences have equipped her with wisdom and maturity to navigate her transition as the new principal.

Different styles, yes. Different opportunities and challenges, yes. And for us at First United Methodist, even greater ways to serve and to learn *how* to be caregivers!

A Move to Year-Round School

We faced a challenge in our volunteer work when Eugene Field began to deal with summer programs and eventually adopted a year-round school calendar. In the early years of the new millennium, we helped set up craft clubs to provide creative learning experiences during the summer months and spring-break periods. We later developed camp programs that offered swimming and fishing to the children. Not all of the children participated in these programs, of course, and we faced the challenge of providing volunteers in months when most volunteer programs go dormant, but we *did* provide both continuity and excellence to the school in these off-season times.

Outfitting Students with Uniforms

Another challenge presented itself when Eugene Field adopted the requirement of school uniforms. Uniforms are a great equalizer, and in a poor community, they help erase the lines between the "haves" and "have-nots." The uniforms eliminated the wearing of gang colors and gang-related symbols.

When we were asked if we might help provide school uniforms, the response at First United Methodist was one word: "Absolutely!" The first year, we raised $12,000 for school uniforms, which meant that every child got *three* brand-new uniforms for free. Those contributions have continued through the years, although the need for our financial giving has lessened. We continue to help when needs arise.

To the delight of school officials and teachers, discipline problems went down by ten percent almost immediately after uniforms were required. Gang talk and gang involvement also dropped.

The Leader in Me Involves The Entire School

In 2012, Principal Dr. Sheila Riley received a grant to implement a program titled *The Leader in Me*, which teaches leadership skills and encourages students to pursue excellence and success both at school and in their neighborhood. The program is a children's version of a course first developed for adults by Stephen Covey.

The Leader in Me[2] focuses on the seven habits listed below. Some of these habits are paraphrased and abbreviated here, but the core principles are well publicized on campus and talked about routinely by teachers and our volunteers:

HABIT 1 — *Be Proactive. "You're in Charge."*

Have a can-do attitude. Don't blame others. Choose your actions, attitude, and friends. Choose to do the right thing even before others tell you to.

HABIT 2 — *Begin with the End in Mind. "Have a Plan."*

Plan ahead and set goals.

HABIT 3 — *Put First Things First. "Work First, Then Play."*

Don't put things off. Set priorities and stick with them.

HABIT 4 — *Think Win-Win. "Everyone Can Win."*

Do things for others. You don't have to put others down. Choose to help others to become a success.

HABIT 5 — *Seek First to Understand, Then Be Understood. "Listen Before You Talk."*

Listen to the ideas and feelings of others. Listen and don't interrupt. Try to see things from the other person's perspective.

HABIT 6 — *Synergize. "Together Is Better."*

Choose to work well with others, even if they are different from you. Work well in groups.

HABIT 7 — *Sharpen the Saw. "Balance Feels Best."*

Eat right, exercise, and get lots of sleep. Spend time with family and friends. Learn in lots of ways and in lots of places.

This program has added some content structure to the work of our mentors, and most of the First United Methodist volunteers are fully on board with the underlying spiritual and Christian-living principles that can be readily folded into mentor/mentee conversations.

Volunteers Have Also Taken Initiatives

While we take our *lead* from the school and do not pursue any activity with which the school disagrees, the school has also responded very enthusiastically to some of our volunteer initiatives.

Parent-Teacher Conference Support. Two of our church members, Chuck and Sherry Ramsay, pioneered an incentive program to encourage greater participation in parent-teacher conferences. They continue to lead a team of volunteers to put together gifts for each student and parent who attends a parent-teacher conference. After the meeting, the students and parents receive a coupon that they bring to the gym, where they can to pick out the gift they want. There are smiles on the faces of the students, the volunteers, and the parents. We know the teachers and principal are probably smiling, too, since participation in the parent-teacher conferences has soared!

A Fishing Day. In a similar way, we had two of our members offer us the use of their property for special events involving Eugene Field students and teachers. Randy and Claudia Imel are the owners of a beautiful property called Five Oaks. The Imels see their property as a gift from God, and they have been quick to share it with community ministries projects and especially Eugene Field. They were the first to host a fishing day for the fifth-grade class, including the gift of a fishing pole to each participating student. One of Randy Imel's unique talents is showing people how to catch fish, so this was a time of great fun for him and for the children. The Imels have also hosted Christmas dinners for the teachers from Eugene Field.

Family Portraits. The idea to take portraits of Eugene Field students with their families originated with Dave Miller with inspiration and support from Creative Life Fellowship. The Fellowship is a group of artists of all kinds— writers, photographers, painters, sculptors—in the One in the Spirit Sunday School class who meet regularly to encourage each others' creative efforts. This idea was definitely God-inspired.

Seventy Eugene Field families turned out to have their pictures taken, dressed in their Sunday best and many in color-coordinated outfits. This was a rare opportunity—budgets for many Eugene Field families didn't include money for family portraits. Volunteer photographers and assistants Dave and Janie Miller, Lyndle and Mary Ellis, John and Shelli Pleasant, Jack and Sondra Reeder, Andy Leithner, and others positioned each family group and got smiles on their faces.

Some weeks later, when families came for the school's Family Picnic in May 2015, the volunteers came with a free portrait package for each family. There was excitement, laughter, and even some grateful tears as the families received their photographs sure to be treasured with pride for many years.

Summer Camp Scholarships. Volunteers initiated a program in 2001 and 2002 to help Eugene Field students attend summer programs at Kanakuk Kamp, Shepherd's Fold, and Camp Loughridge.

In 2005, the Patria Sunday school class, under the leadership of Todd Conklin, sponsored fifty children to attend the Kids Across America (KAA) camp. Todd was in charge of pairing families with the Eugene Field children. He would match them to mirror a sponsor family's children's ages if possible. Todd was First United Methodist's contact with KAA during the three to four years the Patria class sponsored close to fifty students each summer for this camp.

After a hiatus of several years, a volunteer emerged to reinstate the program. Duke Dresser, who had become involved at Eugene Field through the influence of his great friends, Clark and Anne Millspaugh, became the mentor to a young boy named Thomas. Duke made sure Thomas got involved in sports—mostly because Duke believes strongly that sports help keep kids out of trouble and off drugs.

After mentoring Thomas for a year, making sure that the boy played football, and then basketball, and then soccer, he began to think about the upcoming summer. Duke set his mind and heart on getting Thomas to camp. The cost was $150 for six nights, seven days, all meals included, and that was affordable for Duke. He knew the experience would be rewarding for Thomas and that he could count on Thomas being kept busy all day, filled up at meal times, and offered a great night's sleep. KAA had a rule, however, that a child could not go to the camp without a "Kaleo"—an adult over the age of twenty—to help a child in case of injury, homesickness, or disciplinary problems. So Duke sent his adult son Chad to camp with Thomas—and they both had a great time.

The next year, Duke and other church members sponsored more children to go to the camp, and in the summer of 2012, this group sent sixteen children and two Kaleos, and in 2013, eight children and one Kaleo to camp.

The camp is a life-changing event for those who go. They experience Bible study times, Christian group sing-alongs, and great fellowship with other children—all in the name of Jesus.

Company Volunteers. On occasion, our volunteers have also "volunteered" their companies. Brad Camp is the president of a company called HiCORP, which first became involved with First United Methodist more than fourteen years ago. The first year, HiCORP had only about fifteen employees, but seven of them partnered with First United Methodist to become mentors to children at Eugene Field.

About six years ago, HiCORP focused on the second-grade class at Eugene Field. They met with the teachers to help provide school supplies, Christmas gifts, and to host parties … for the entire grade! At year's end, they host a "Reading Bombdiggity Blow-Out All-You-Can-Eat Ice Cream Party" to send the second-graders off to third grade in style.

Brad has said, "I am convinced that Eugene Field has changed HiCORP—many of our employees have moved from being takers to givers. The involvement at the school is part of our identity now—we give, we serve."

"Invisible" Workers. There are some volunteers at the church who specialize in putting together training and orientation packets, hosting a Sunday lunch to introduce church members to the volunteer opportunities at Eugene Field, recruiting volunteers at community ministries sign-up events, speaking to reporters about possible articles, and other promotional and public-relations functions. These volunteers may or may not have direct face-to-face relationships with the children at Eugene Field. They are valuable to the ministry nonetheless!

And More! These examples of service are just that—examples. Our volunteers have been versatile, eager, and extremely effective in the ministry they have taken on. For the most part, they seem to have fun in the outreaches they undertake. There truly is an atmosphere of joy and fulfillment at the school.

Excitement Shared for the New School Campus

Eugene Field Elementary School was built in 1922, and needless to say, the buildings were in bad shape by the 1990s.

In 1996, a $6.9 million bond was passed to build a new Eugene Field, but with declining enrollment, Tulsa Public Schools wouldn't spend money on a new school if they thought they might have to shut its doors almost immediately.

By 2004, the population at Eugene Field had risen to three hundred students and it became clear that Eugene Field Elementary School wasn't going to collapse. Tulsa Public Schools moved forward with plans for a brand-new state-of-the-art school. We at First United Methodist were as excited as the principal and teachers. After all, this had become our school, too.

The principal, Cindi Hemm, took a rather bold but creative move once the beams were up and the classroom spaces identifiable. She took her faculty over to the new building for a walkthrough after school hours. The faculty and administrators armed themselves with yellow hard hats, permanent markers, and pages of Scripture, and as they walked through the framed-in structure, they prayed a prayer of dedication over the building, including a petition for the Lord's safety, and then they wrote Scripture verses on every wall, floor, and door facing.

Those who did this knew that what they wrote would be covered by drywall, carpet, and paint. Even so, it is still a good thing for us to remember as volunteers from First United Methodist that we are doing our volunteer service in a place that has been dedicated to true mission service and has Scripture embedded in its structure and foundation—perhaps even more "hidden" verses of Scripture than in most churches!

A School "Resurrection"

For years, Eugene Field was in decline. The aging school building was uninviting and located in an isolated area. A neighborhood history of generational poverty had resulted in a high mobility rate. Declining conditions in neighborhood public housing became the focus of the school and the staff. Lack of neighborhood resources gave people all the more reason to want to leave. By 2003, Eugene Field was on the brink of closure. Enrollment was at an all-time low of 170 students and test scores were among the worst in the state. The school had a 97 percent poverty rate and a 97 percent rate of mobility (the number of times a child moves to a different school).

Within the school, morale was low. A number of the teachers did not know how to deal with children who lived in extreme poverty, and they tended to adopt a "just doing my job" mindset until they could find a way to be transferred to a more prosperous, safe, and educationally excellent environment.

That is no longer the case. Local agencies likewise took notice of the neighborhood decline and made a commitment to revitalization. More resources began to flow into the community—including strong compassionate leadership. Teachers received pertinent training and support and encouragement. The school now has an enrollment of more than 350 students and is increasingly regarded for excellence and stability. In 2008, Community Action Project Tulsa opened the Early Childhood Education Center on West 22nd St., adding a vital resource to the Eugene Field neighborhood.

With the establishment of a reading sufficiency initiative in Oklahoma for the 2013–2014 academic year, all third-grade students were required to be reading on grade level or risk being retained in third grade. Eugene Field had only one third-grader who failed the reading test (and that likely was owing to his being absent for seventy-six days that academic year). I believe there is a direct correlation to our partnership with Eugene Field. Along with the Reading

Partners program volunteers, we helped produce one of the best third-grade teaching teams in our school district.

The school this past year reached the 70 percent threshold for proficiency schoolwide. This is up from 52 percent two years ago.

All of the goals in *The Leader in Me* program were successfully implemented and the school held its first "leadership day" planned and performed entirely by the students.

Programs called *Read 180* and *System 44* were successfully implemented, and the upper-grade students showed tremendous growth.

Since 2015, fourth through sixth grades have had access to a research-based program called *Brainology*. This program presents a growth mindset to students, something that students in poverty often lack. Impoverished students often think that if they can't do something right away, they must not be smart enough. A growth mindset teaches that effort and hard work can increase learning ability.

All of these are signs that Eugene Field is moving forward ... and upward.

More and more leadership roles are being provided for students at the school, and we are happy to help!

ENDNOTES

1   I recommend to you *Miracle on Southwest Boulevard* by Cindi Hemm, published by Westbow Press in 2011.

2   Stephen Covey, *The Leader in Me* (NY: Simon and Schuster, 2008). For more information go to www.theleaderinme.org

*The names of the campers have been changed to protect their identity.

6

Reaching Beyond the School into the Neighboring Community

As a minister, I am always encouraged any time I see an individual or a group of people move from surviving to thriving. That is what I see at Eugene Field. The school is no longer struggling just to stay open.

A major part of the change at Eugene Field was and is the innovative, challenging, and affirming environment that has been created for both students and families in the school's *neighborhood*. I am extremely pleased that First United Methodist had a major role in changing this part of our city.

Moving Beyond the Schoolyard

It was obvious to us from our first day of adopting Eugene Field Elementary School that we also faced a serious challenge in ministering to the community that surrounded the school. As much as we needed to learn about the students—and the faculty and administrators—to which God had called us, we needed to learn about *their families* and *the neighborhood* that influenced them so profoundly.

We had a lot to discover.

A School and a Neighborhood in Crisis

Eugene Field Elementary School is located in Tulsa, Oklahoma, in an area generally called "the west side." It technically is the western area of the city, as it is west of the Arkansas River, which runs north to south through Tulsa.

West Tulsa has a longstanding identity as the section of the city that is a little more "country" than south Tulsa and more "white" than north Tulsa and east Tulsa (which have large African American and Hispanic populations). A friend of mine once said this about west Tulsa: "It's the part of town where you'll find pickup trucks with gun racks, train whistles, and diners with massive platters of delicious chicken-fried steak, mashed potatoes, and gravy … and waitresses that will call you 'dawlin' and keep your coffee cup full."

Over the years West Tulsa became a section of the city that has struggled with poverty and crime. Eugene Field is bordered generally by two oil refineries, the busy thoroughfare of Southwest Boulevard (Route 66), and the river. It is a little oasis of potential in an area that is generally perceived as old and run down.

In the early 1900s, the area became the location where the oil refineries built low-cost housing for the oil workers who were flocking to Tulsa. Through the years, the neighborhood was plagued with devastating floods (before the Keystone Dam curtailed flooding of the Arkansas River), destructive fires, and widespread contagious disease outbreaks. Nevertheless, the people who lived there were proud to call West Tulsa home. An amusement park called The Sunset Plunge was the centerpiece of the community, located in a beautiful grove of ancient cottonwood trees. When the amusement park closed and the cottonwood trees were uprooted, the area slowly fell into decline.

The most devastating blow to the community came when an urban renewal project in the 1970s made what most now believe to be a misguided move to clean up the area. City officials ordered that old buildings be bulldozed and barrack-style apartment buildings be constructed. The once close-knit community was dispersed in the process, and the commercial district that served the area was almost destroyed.

By the dawn of the new millennium, the closest quality grocery store required a half-day, round-trip bus ride, and area residents often were limited to shopping at a small convenience store that charged $7 for a half-gallon of milk and had no fresh vegetables or fruit.

Creating an Identity as a Community School

A little more than a decade ago, Eugene Field announced that it was going to become a "community school." At that time, the term *community school* had come to refer to a school that attempted to serve the whole child by expanding the focus beyond academics to include a wide range of health and social services, youth and community development, and real-world learning.[1]

The hope was that if a child's basic needs were met and the child began to see himself as having a safe, supportive, and stable environment, the student's learning would be improved. The strength of a family and the health of the broader community were perceived as being vital to a child's intellectual development. We at First United Methodist could certainly embrace such an idea.

The constant challenge, of course, is to strike a balance between helping and enabling. We saw our role as helping the school become a social center and a mechanism for helping people from the community find ways to resolve their social needs. The goal became, and continues to be, for both students and their parents to see the school as a safe and positive place to be.

We helped with this process in several major ways.

End-of-the-Month Community Dinners

The Eugene Field students had a serious hunger problem. Many of the parents were on welfare, and they often struggled to put even a basic meal on the table for their children. We stepped up to sponsor free community dinners at the end of each month, which was the time food stamps ran out, family funds had been spent, and the need for food was the greatest. Dan and Terry Young were the champions for this outreach, which started in 2004, and they only recently passed the torch of leadership to Don and Julie Porter and their six children, Colyn, Bailey, Keegan, Gentry, Larkin, and Beckham.

The last Friday of every month, members of First United Methodist began to invade the Eugene Field campus with food. Not only did they provide the food and serve the meals, but they also spent time listening to the those who came and volunteered to pray for those who expressed a willingness to receive prayer.

The event now involves 200–400 people. It is a mainstay community involvement event. It is a social and spiritual event, far more than a feeding event. Recently, Growing Together, a community development partnership, asked to partner with First Methodist in hosting the community dinners. Volunteers from West Tulsa United Methodist Church and Harvest Church have also come alongside First.

Those who have volunteered for this ministry have told me repeatedly that they receive even more than they give—that the people are not only receptive to the meals but *thankful* for them, and that in the years of going to the school on a monthly basis, there has been no need to call security or the police. The mealtimes are peaceful times, another active example of school and community coming together.

Bingo is played after dinner. The prizes are household items—from food to large jigsaw puzzles to diapers to cleaning supplies to paper goods. Various grade choirs perform during dinner, singing about the principles they have learned through *The Leader in Me* curriculum.

Global Gardens Provide Food and Teaching Opportunities

The planting of a community garden was yet another way to help provide food for the impoverished Eugene Field neighborhood. Once again, God sent a champion for the cause.

Heather Oakley met Todd Rippy at First United Methodist when they were both young teens. She and Todd went on a mission trip with the youth department at First United Methodist to work at an orphanage in Mexico. That experience solidified Heather's sense of mission, which would frame her future.

Heather spent four months in an East African boys' orphanage learning and befriending impoverished orphans who worked on the farm to pay for their schooling. She saw the tremendous impact that planting and growing food could have on an impoverished child. Growing food truly was a way *out* of poverty.

Heather attended the University of Oklahoma to study botany and then worked in Florida with low-income children before she moved to New York to work as a science teacher and attend graduate school at Columbia University. She taught school in Harlem and there she planted her first "Global Garden," launching her dream into reality.

Heather returned to Tulsa for a visit in 2006, with no intention of staying in the city. She had plans to take her Global Gardens nonprofit program to a developing nation, but all that changed dramatically when she fell in love with and married her childhood friend, Todd Rippy.

Heather was introduced to Eugene Field by her parents, Pam and Shelby Oakley, who had volunteered as mentors at the school for a year. Heather shared with the principal her dream of teaching children about planting, science, peace, healthy lifestyles, good eating habits, and cultural diversity, and she immediately was given an opportunity to do all of the above.

The first garden was tilled and planted on land adjacent to the school in April 2007, and the results were amazing. Not only did the garden produce food items for the families of the children, but the garden itself sent a strong message to the community that the school valued health and real community development. It did not go unnoticed, of course, that *every child* in the fifth grade, the main grade involved in the planting, cultivating, and harvesting of the garden, passed the fifth-grade science proficiency test for the first time in the school's history!

Students took great pride in "their" gardens—each grade was allotted a specific area to plan, plant, cultivate, and harvest. They loved taking home the produce they had grown to their parents.

From a broader perspective, the garden has provided a safe, friendly, productive, positive place for people in the community to meet. The children and their families can be found in the garden area throughout the growing season—often late in the day, as well as on Saturdays and Sundays. The garden has become something of a community center for the greater neighborhood—one that has the potential to benefit every resident.

The academic spillover effect went beyond science class. After the first garden was planted, student scores in all areas rose to become some of the best scores in the entire state. Both student attendance and parent involvement increased to unprecedented levels.

The Eugene Field Global Garden also meant a new opportunity for First United Methodist volunteers. Members of the church have helped provide the garden with tools and garden gloves, fruit trees, and mulch. A long wish list of things related to the gardening project are offered as contribution suggestions annually.

The Westside Harvest Market Serves an Unserved Neighborhood

It was a natural progression—at least in retrospect—that a community garden might be located next to a store that would sell their produce.

Clark Millspaugh and his wife, Anne, volunteered as mentors at Eugene Field for a number of years, beginning in the late 1990s. Then, in 2009, the Millspaughs became the champions of a new outreach that changed the community in a dramatic way.

One day after retiring and selling his oil-related business, Clark paid a visit to the principal's office, and there he saw a child asleep in a beanbag chair. He asked about the little girl and was told, "She is homeless, very abused, and hungry. We are trying to teach her to read and write, but in the meantime, all she is trying to do is survive."[2] Clark reached down and patted the sleeping child on the back, and as he did, he felt her spine protruding from her back, and he began to cry. He asked, "What can I do to help make things a little better for these children?"[3]

The principal said, "These people need a grocery store, some place within walking distance of their homes that has affordable groceries."

Clark drove around the school and through the adjacent neighborhood and later called a group of investors together. They bought two vacant buildings for $250,000 and used another $250,000 to renovate them. Then they created a nonprofit organization to run a grocery store.

For a number of years, the reason cited for no grocery store in the area was repeatedly this: "It's too dangerous." Nobody wanted to take the financial risk or to establish a business with a cash register in a high-crime neighborhood.

Sometimes faith needs to fly in the face of reason—especially if there are people who are willing to find a new "reasonable" way to provide good food to a neighborhood for a fair price.

The solution that Clark and his team came up with was genius, in my opinion. It was truly a God-style win-win solution that the new grocery store was established as a nonprofit that provided more than milk and bread to the customers. The store, as initially designed and constructed, also housed a kitchen classroom—established to help children and residents acquire nutrition information along with cooking skills—and a prayer room that was initially open 24/7, plus offices for the Global Gardens leaders. The grocery store was named the Westside Harvest Market, and at the time of its founding, it was the only market in the area that was a source for fresh produce.

The prayer room was a major motivating factor for Millspaugh in the founding of the market. On a long flight on a mission trip to Kazakhstan, Clark read a book that changed his life, *Red Moon Rising*, by Pete Greig and Dave Roberts. The book tells about the power of prayer and describes 24/7 prayer rooms called "Boiler Rooms," where "the fires of intercession are stoked" for miracles.

The prayer room was a place of peace and quiet—something that is often very rare in an impoverished neighborhood. The prayer room had comfortable couches and chairs, gentle background praise music, and soft lighting. There were Bibles to read and places that invited quiet meditation.

The market has changed its policies and procedures about prayer through the years, but prayer is still a vital part of what makes this market a genuine *ministry*, not just a store.

The store does accept food stamps and is located next to the Eugene Field property. It is open six days a week. It carries milk, bread, vegetables and fruit, and other wholesome food at affordable prices. In many ways, it has become a Christ-honoring place every bit as gospel-oriented as any church.

The Westside Harvest Market is a place where the produce *not* used by classroom children and their families is available for sale to the public. Community and school were linked in a new way.

Part of the Global Gardens' work, as well as the Harvest Market's ministry, is the teaching kitchen. In this kitchen, children learn how to measure ingredients, follow recipes, bake, and serve quality wholesome food. It is amazing to see how thrilled elementary-aged children can be about making zucchini bread and blueberry muffins from scratch, and how much they enjoy eating what they bake and sharing their baked goods with others.

In 2010, The Burgh Community Church moved into the neighborhood, being housed in the Harvest Market. The Good Samaritan Mobile Health Clinic was reinstated, setting up in the Harvest Market parking lot every Wednesday. GED classes began to be offered, and the Junior League of Tulsa started offering cooking classes. The next year, The Burgh Community Church became Harvest Community Church, and Clark asked the church to assume the leadership responsibility for the store.

Day Spring Counseling Services joined the Harvest team in 2013 and an enterprise known as Westside Boat Works led by FUMC member Gary Edmondson also began.

The mission of The Harvest, which includes the Harvest Community Church and The Harvest Market, is to restore, repair and rebuild. It is a vibrant ongoing ministry that serves the neighborhood in multiple practical ways.

Providing Homes for the Poor

First United Methodist volunteers have assisted in a number of Habitat for Humanity and Rebuilding Together Tulsa projects. One of our construction projects was one the volunteers dubbed an "Extreme Miracle Makeover." They remodeled a home for a couple who had adopted several children. They listed the things they did:

- Tore out all the carpet, bad ceilings, window air-conditioning units
- Replaced the flooring, both hardwood and carpet, installed central heating and air-conditioning, and new electric and light fixtures
- Installed new kitchen appliances, refinished cabinets, and put in new kitchen countertops
- Installed a new washer and dryer
- Painted the entire interior and exterior
- Repaired outside roofing and siding
- Installed window boxes and shutters
- Provided plants for the flower boxes and put sod in the back yard
- Installed a new fence and gate
- Put in new drapes and shower curtains
- Decorated the boys bedroom with Disney Cars bedspreads and curtains
- Decorated the girls bedroom with Disney Princess bedspreads and curtains

All of the materials and labor were donated, and in the words of volunteer leaders Sam and Norma Hollinger, "The look on the faces of the family members is worth all the hard work."

ENDNOTES

1   Jamie Richert Jones, "A Community's School," *TulsaPeople*, February 2014, 54. http://www.tulsapeople.com/Tulsa-People/February-2014/A-communitys-school

2   Cindi Hemm, <u>Miracle on Southwest Boulevard</u> (Bloomington, IN: Westbow Press, 2011) 106.

3   Ibid., 107.

7

Memories from Our Eugene Field Scrapbook

Facts and statistics are good, but in my opinion, the really great insight into our work at Eugene Field is found in the pages of our scrapbook of notes and memories shared by volunteers and teachers. I offer you just a sampling.

"A Place Where God's Love Can Be Expressed Openly"

A little girl named Sophie was eight years old when I first met her. She had been in eight foster homes during her life. Even so, she was a ray of sunshine and had a smile that could light up an entire room. She was a gentle soul who seemed to have been given a gift of supernatural joy. One winter morning, she came to school without a coat. Her cheeks were bright red, and she was shivering in a way that let me know she was bone-cold. I asked her where her coat was. She said she couldn't find it. I had a deep intuition that there was no coat to find.

I brought Sophie's situation to the attention of one of the leading volunteers from First United Methodist, and by the time the day ended, Sophie had a warm coat and a small sack of nutritious food to take home to her foster family.

A few weeks later, Sophie came to school with an adult I had not met before. Sophie was being placed in yet another foster home. She said, "Mrs. Graham, I just had to come and say goodbye, so I begged until they brought me." This was an unusual moment. So often, children living in poverty never get to say good-bye before they are moved, or their parents move suddenly and take them from our midst. Sophie continued, "Mrs. Graham, would you just hold my hand and let me walk around the school and see it one last time to say goodbye?" We did just that. As we parted, it was my turn to say something. "Sophie, Mrs. Graham may never see you again, but remember one thing. God loves you, and He has given you the gift of joy. No matter what happens, Sophie, you hang on to that because you touch the lives of everyone you meet and bring sunshine into their day. Remember that God has a plan for your life, and no matter what happens, He is faithful." Every child in the class then stood up to hug Sophie before she walked away with her new adult caregiver.

Of course I cried. Who wouldn't? But they were also tears of thanksgiving that I am working in a place where God's love is allowed to be expressed.

The volunteers with whom I worked from First United Methodist were passionate, authentic, and faithful. They had a big role in my returning to active church attendance and a renewal of my faith. I can never say thank you enough.

—*Angela Graham Callahan, Site Administrative Manager, Tulsa Public Schools*

"Put Together for a Reason"

I have been a mentor to a precious ten-year-old girl for more than four years. I first met Ryan when she was in the first grade, and we later talked about how nervous we were at our first meeting. *Would she like me? Would I like her?* We quickly got over those concerns and discovered we were a perfect fit.

Our relationship has grown stronger with each year as we have helped each other through some difficult times. Ryan is a delight; she is smart, cute, fun and funny, and passionate with her love for the Global Gardens. We spent time together doing the things all good friends do. We eat lunch, play games, laugh at silly jokes; we have cried together, and we always pray together. I believe Ryan came into my life for a reason, and I like to think that God has a purpose for me in her life. I may be her mentor, but she is my joy.

—*Jan Sweeney, First United Methodist volunteer*

"I Can't Wait to Go Back"

Erin didn't know why she was called out of class and was a little hesitant when she got to the principal's office. Jeremy explained that she had been assigned a mentor and introduced me. The principal then suggested that she show me around the school.

Erin flashed the biggest smile I've ever seen, took my hand, and skipped down the hall, calling out to everyone we met, "I've got a mentor! This is my mentor!" We saw the music room, the art room, the gym, and the library. We went to the cafeteria, where she highly recommended the chicken spaghetti. It was delicious.

Erin talked nonstop. Some of the things I learned: The fur coat in her locker is actually faux fur. She didn't go to overnight camp because she isn't nocturnal and they do stuff all night. Erin is a tomboy, but her mother isn't because she wears makeup and necklaces. She wants to be a veterinarian. A person can wear pants that are five sizes too big if she has a very tight pink belt. Even more fun than shooting the paper off your straw would be for your mentor to come every day. What an experience! I can't wait to go back.

—*Jennith Moncrief, First United Methodist volunteer*

"Ministry Isn't Always Tidy"

I first became connected with a third-grader named Darian, who was above his grade level in spelling and wanted to be a basketball player when he grew up. We usually spent our lunch hour out on the playground playing whatever game or sport Darian and his friends wanted to play.

Over time, I met Darian's mother and little brother Blaze. Darian's mom was comfortable with my wife, Kelly, and me taking her sons to Tulsa Drillers games and, later, participating in the youth sports leagues at the First United Methodist Youth and Family Center. Darian also participated in a spring-break mission trip sponsored by the church.

Darian struggled with his home life—a single mother, an absent dad, a house in desperate need of repairs, never enough money, and a constant temptation to gravitate to the wrong kinds of friends. We stayed in touch through the years. During his sophomore year in high school, Darian changed schools and did get in with the wrong crowd. He eventually dropped out of school, which broke my heart. His brother Blaze developed problems of his own.

I'd like to be able to wrap all this up neatly and say the story has a happy ending. But the reality is, at least for me, ministry isn't always neat and tidy. A lot of the time it is risky and a bit chaotic. But the story isn't finished! Darian did eventually earn his GED, and I know that Jesus is still tugging on the hearts of these young men. I'm there when they want to pick up the phone and call me— which Darian does from time to time, and always on Father's Day! Do I regret getting involved? Not for a second.

—*Tom Junk, First United Methodist volunteer*

"A Birthday Party for Children Who Don't Receive Them"

Like most mothers, I have become acutely aware that turning five is a big event in a child's life. At that age, a mother is starting to accept the truth that her child is growing up. And the child is acutely aware that a birthday means games, treats, and toys.

The day before my son turned five, he announced to me that he had invited his entire kindergarten class to our house for a party! This declaration came as quite a shock to me, and I was frantic in making the calls and plans necessary to provide the party he had planned without consulting either of his parents.

After the party, I sat down with my son and informed him that he must *not* invite groups of people to our home without telling me in advance about his idea. I also tried to reinforce to him the idea that there are many children in the world who do not have parents who can give them parties such as the one he had hosted. He replied, "No way. Everybody gets a birthday party with presents, cake, and friends." It took several conversations on this subject before he acknowledged that I *might* be right. Then he asked with simplicity and bluntness: "Well, what are you going to do about that, Mom?"

My son's reluctance to believe that birthdays were not the privilege of many children set me to thinking. What might it mean to a child in an impoverished home to have a birthday party? I went with this question to my church. I knew about the volunteer efforts of First United Methodist members at Eugene Field Elementary School. I asked the church leadership if we might sponsor a collective birthday party for the students and use our newly built Family Life Center to host the parties. Cake and decorations would be abundant. A gift for each child would be given. Perhaps the party might be hosted on a monthly or quarterly basis, perhaps by grade level.

The words of Jesus rang in my ears: "Let the little children come to me, and do not hinder them, for the kingdom of heaven belongs to such as these" (Matthew 19:14). I had a strong sense that I wasn't only seeking to give a birthday party to a child who might not otherwise have one, but that I would be doing something that pleased Jesus.

—Kim Tryon-Grider, First United Methodist volunteer

"I Reluctantly Agreed"

I started helping at the Big Bucks Store in 2003. Most of the items made available to the children were clothing, toiletries, and school supplies. We quickly discovered that books did not "sell" well, so we sold books and toys together—a two-for-one deal. That way, we knew the child would be getting something helpful to reading skills, even if the child was reading resistant.

When the store's leader, Sharon McMahon, moved to Oklahoma City after her husband was transferred there, I reluctantly took over responsibility for the store. I don't consider myself a natural leader, but with much prayer, I took on the responsibility and began shopping garage sales in earnest!

We have faced a number of unexpected challenges through the years. Like the time we discovered that rats had invaded our storage closet and store area. My assistant, who became my co-partner in leading the store, Jill Miller, jumped in and organized all of our merchandise into clear storage tubs, and after sanitizing and cleaning the area thoroughly, she set up a plan for storing many of our contributed items at her family barn. That allowed us to solicit contributed items year round and avoid the holiday rush.

The Big Bucks Store had started in one kindergarten classroom and required setup and teardown each time the store was open. We eventually were given both rooms of a trailer for the store, and I'm not sure the principal knew it, but her decision to give us that space was a direct answer to prayer.

We monitor the number of students in the store at any time. Usually, a group of about six students is given about five minutes to shop. This means they must make rather quick buying decisions.

We have tried a number of things—we have had volunteers show the children how to wrap their purchases for gift-giving, we have given a piece of candy as a bonus to students who earn all four available Bucks in a given earning period, and in 2013, at Principal Riley's suggestion, we started an area of the store for parent volunteers to shop for items moms might enjoy—from scented soaps to lotions to gift wrap.

The store gives so many opportunities for life lessons. Children discover the value of saving for a new toy or gift item rather than buying a trinket or candy or balloon that has little lasting value. They learn manners and shopping etiquette—putting back items they have handled, looking their elders in the eye, and communicating their requests with respect.

We have experienced what we regard as genuine miracles in supplying children with some of the things they need. Not long ago, we had a boy in the store who was in need of a coat, and we happened to have a brand-new coat in exactly his size in our donation box! Two weeks ago, we had a boy ask if we had a particular game. I didn't know, but I went to check, and discovered that we had precisely that game, complete with an instruction book! Another boy asked if we had any Legos. Again, I went to our restock closet and found a new small Lego set that was priced at just the amount this boy had to spend.

I have also enjoyed interaction with the children's parents. A while back, one of our volunteers made soup for us, and we had some leftover soup that I offered to a sixth-grader named Jennifer who came by after school to say hello. She gladly accepted the soup, and I drove her home. Her mother invited me into their apartment, and as soon as I walked in, I saw a cross on the wall that this girl had purchased with Big Bucks as a gift. I commented on it, and her mother told me how much she loved the gifts her daughter brought home to her. It was a blessing to see how the store was having an impact out in the real world where children such as Jennifer live. I had a warm feeling that this cross is something that Jennifer sees every day, and whether she thinks about it or not, it is a reminder to her of the love she receives from those of us who volunteer at her school.

We have also discovered that the teachers increasingly use Big Bucks as classroom incentives—they reward good behavior and classroom performance, and the students are seeing the direct connection between academic performance, attendance, good behavior, and Big Bucks. It seems extremely valuable to me that students are motivated toward *good* accomplishments rather than reprimanded for bad behavior.

I was asked recently if we ever have shoplifters. We do. The students who put items in their pockets without paying for them are usually caught, and we use this as an opportunity to give a lesson on sin and forgiveness. They lose their shopping privileges for an extended time, but they also know that we *want* them back as our "customers." Our hope is that the way we handle shoplifting might keep a student from a more serious crime down the line.

We also had a break-in a couple of summers ago. Very inexpensive items were taken. The two students involved were caught and lost their shopping privileges for several months. Again, we put our emphasis on forgiveness, and God seemed to honor that—we have nicer jewelry and higher quality items in the store now than before the break-in.

On a very personal level, volunteering at the Big Bucks Store has enabled me to have a wonderful friendship with my co-leader, Jill. It has also given me wonderful hours with my mother, who often comes to help with the store. And it has been a blessing to my daughter Allison. Allison was fourteen years old when I first volunteered to help with the Big Bucks Store. Allison came to help on several occasions. She was hired in 2013 to teach in exactly the grade she desired … at Eugene Field! My younger daughter Katie now comes to the school occasionally to read with some of the girls in Allison's classroom!

Since the Big Bucks Store is located outside the classrooms and is supported fully by First United Methodist, we are able to have a big sign that says FUMC LOVES YOU! hanging in our window, and we also are free to pray with students who want prayer and give a hug to any child who wants a hug. We usually are able to hand out a small card or bookmark every Christmas that tells the Christmas story to the students. These are bonus opportunities for those of us who volunteer. We don't think of ourselves as running a store but rather as having a ministry that we believe will give God glory!

—*Debi Emery, First United Methodist volunteer*

"A New World of Teaching"

I went to college with the intention of becoming a secondary math teacher like my father. All I needed to complete my undergraduate degree was a student teaching practicum with eighth-grade students. The reality was, those eighth-graders were tougher than I was. I lasted only two days as a student teacher.

The upshot of that experience was a change of major, a couple extra years of undergraduate study, and a new direction for my life—or so I thought. I went on to graduate school, entered the petroleum industry, and never looked back.

Then, as a father with two young daughters about to enter preschool and kindergarten, I had to confront my past failures. The kindergarten teacher asked for parent volunteers to read to the children. My wife, who was a teacher and principal, made it clear that she thought I should be one of those volunteers. Memories of my classroom experiences with those eighth-graders came flooding back. I swallowed hard and agreed to be a reading mentor.

Right from the start, I found myself thrown into a new world of literature and art I didn't know existed. It was a joyful time reading to those kids. And then, almost as soon as it had started, my children grew up and moved on to second grade, where parental mentors were no longer requested or required. I assumed my mentoring days were over.

Little did I know that God had a different plan for me. Almost immediately my wife and I got involved with teaching Sunday school to the children at our church. We taught for ten years. At the end of that time, I began to think again that my teaching days were over. Then Emily Renberg, FUMC's volunteer coordinator, suggested that I volunteer at the school a day or two a week, but I was ready for a break from mentoring and declined. Emily was very persistent. After two years of Emily and the Holy Spirit speaking to me, I finally agreed to visit the school and see what all the fuss was about. I was hooked immediately.

The first student assigned to me was a quiet, shy, first-grader named José. We were together for the next three years. José had an interesting family story not dissimilar to that of most of the kids at Eugene Field. After developing some trust, he shared his life in small bits and pieces over our time together. When we first began our journey, his father was released from prison and immediately deported back to their family home in central Mexico. After his father's release, José traveled each summer to visit his father in Mexico. We were never certain if he would return for the fall semester or even if he would be allowed back in the States. It was not unusual for José to randomly show up in the middle of the fall session.

His mother was a domestic worker who spoke very little English. She had divorced José's father after he was sent to prison. His older brother was in constant trouble: he had dropped out of middle school and became associated with a gang. The older brother was eventually rounded up and sent to live with their grandmother in Missouri. Despite all of this instability, José was hard working, well mannered, and an avid student.

At the end of our third year together, José was entering the third grade, and it was time for me to step aside. I continued to mentor younger students primarily with needs in reading skills. However, José and I stayed in touch over the next two years. When José was in the fifth grade at Eugene Field, his mother was killed in a drug-related incident that started when the apartment next door blew up. Since there were no family members living in Tulsa, José was sent to live with his grandmother, who had earlier taken in his older brother. Unfortunately, I never had a chance to speak with him before he left. I have to trust that God is working out *His* plan for this young man's life. I would hope that he is enrolled somewhere for college.

What I do know is that God wants us to plant seeds and trust Him to do the growing of them into a harvest of His choosing. Over the thirteen years I have been mentoring, I have discovered that most of the students at Eugene Field have similar stories—a parent in prison, divorce, separation from family members, life with a grandparent, multiple step-brothers or sisters, abuse, poverty, or some combination of the above. However, these kids are tough and resilient, and they are as much an inspiration to me as I could ever hope to be to them.

—Stacy Clark, First United Methodist volunteer

"A Multi-Decade Commitment"

I first met Lina when she was in third grade at Eugene Field. Lina spoke Spanish at home, and my main role as her mentor was to help her with her English and her favorite subject, math. Even after Lina's parents moved to another school district, I maintained the relationship. My husband and I brought Lina to church, and we also volunteered together at Eugene Field birthday parties. By the time Lina graduated from high school, she was a recognized honor student and had 250 hours of community service!

My husband Richard had met brothers Rayden and Kamari through the Wyldlife program at Clinton Middle School. Richard was the coach of the MACBA basketball team. Even after both brothers moved on to Webster High School, they often joined us at church, and they helped with work at our ranch, painting fences, cleaning stalls, and helping move heavy loads.

Neither Richard nor I consider Lina, Rayden, and Kamari to be anything other than family. We are as enthusiastic about their futures as we are about the futures of our own children. That's what mentoring does!

—*Gayla Dixon, First United Methodist volunteer*

ENDNOTES

*The names of the students have been changed to protect their identity.

8

Taking on the Broader Issue
of Poverty

The Good Samaritan was a dying victim. The need was urgent, obvious, and could be addressed in a fairly straightforward manner.

There is another type of person, however, that we frequently find on life's road. That person is not the victim of a crime but of something just as hurtful and deadly. It is the person trapped in poverty, often but not always homeless.

I learned this in a vivid way in 1985 when I lived in Aberdeen, Scotland, where I was the co-director of a Teen Challenge ministry branch.

Every day, I took a bus from the outskirts of the city into the city center, where our office was located. The bus made many stops, and I quickly learned that my stop was in front of the grocery store and electronics store. That usually meant I could have a few moments of window shopping before I walked around the corner to enter the YMCA, where our office was located.

One cold and blustery morning, I rounded the corner to see a street person, probably homeless, bundled up and propped up against the wall. He was sound asleep. It occurred to me that there was quite a bit of foot traffic on that street, so a number of people had likely seen this man and had simply chosen to let him continue to sleep. Quite a few people had offices in the YMCA building, and a significant number of young people used the YMCA as a hangout. This man was apparently not bothered by the street noise or close-by foot traffic, and those who walked by him weren't bothered by his presence. Nobody had awakened him. Nobody had asked him to leave.

It is also true that none of us had asked him if we might *help* him find a more comfortable, warmer place to sleep. In a much broader sense, none of us had asked if we might help him find a more fulfilling, purposeful, and rewarding life.

Of all the people I met and all the experiences I had in Aberdeen while I was there, this man asleep on our stoop is among my most vivid memories.

There are few who would argue that this was a man in need—a fellow traveler on life's journey who was a likely candidate for help.

Through the years, I have had dramatic encounters with other people who seemed to be victims in need.

One Sunday morning, as I was preaching during a worship service, the front door of the sanctuary opened, and a man walked down the center aisle and sat on the front pew. As I was preaching about compassion, the man got up and walked up the steps to the pulpit. He extended his arm upwards toward me; the congregation froze. An usher came forward and escorted the man out and offered him a cup of coffee. As I returned to my sermon a wave of compassion overwhelmed me to the point of tears. A person in need was in front of all of us that morning.

A short time later, my nephew Asher Cole told me that he had been throwing cardboard boxes into the dumpster outside our sanctuary and had hit a homeless man asleep in the dumpster! He was as disconcerted by that encounter as many of our church members had been that Sunday morning.

In my heart, of course, I know how I feel about those who are overwhelmed by poverty or who are homeless. I feel compassion for them—deep and abiding. Even so, I am always surprised by their sudden appearance in my life or the lives of my loved ones. As many people I know, I'm not always sure what to do, or know where to begin in assisting.

The homeless man asleep on the sidewalk in Aberdeen was the recipient of apathy. None of us took even the simplest action, asking, "Is there something I might do to help you?"

I feel sure that my colleagues and I all assumed to some degree that this man's answer to the question would be "No." But we can never be sure of that. We didn't ask.

Countless people today see other people they believe to be in need and do nothing. They are the ones that people in community ministries programs usually try to jolt into action.

There are also a number of people who see people in need and rush in to help, not fully knowing if the help they are rendering is the *best* help that might be given or even if the people in need *want* help from others.

We *must* ask. We *must* extend the courtesy of asking before we rush headlong into the project *we* think is needed. It is the first and foremost rule of helping.

Asking for Permission to Help

We must begin all ministry to the poor by asking simply, "How might I help you?"

Embedded in this question is a concern that we are also wise to address as we embark on volunteer ministry to help the needy: *To what degree do we perceive the needy person is responsible for their condition or for asking others to help?*

In my experience over the years, there are countless people who have very little role in the troubles they experience or the condition in which they find themselves. Many are victims of circumstances far beyond their control and certainly not in the realm of their desire. Over time, many of them adapt to the misery and poverty in which they find themselves. All of their energy is taken up by efforts to survive—there is no energy or creative ability left over to pursue a path that might lead out of poverty. As one person said, "They are so busy working to get welfare checks or do minimum wage jobs that they do not have the energy or time to get training, look for other work, or even *explore* the idea that a better life might be possible."

We also must be aware that poverty does not remove pride from the equation. A caregiver might assume that all poor people have been so humbled by their circumstances that they have no reluctance to ask for help. That isn't always true, and we must always approach the needy person with respect. A caring, compassionate heart is *not* a heart filled with pity or any form of condemnation. I always encourage our volunteers, "Go into the relationship assuming that God has something for you to do, something for you to learn, and something for you to give. Never assume *anything* about the other person without asking the person what you might do to help. You don't need to know their life history or anything about their circumstances. You simply need to learn whether the person *wants* your help and in what form."

Ultimately, we must explore within our own hearts and in our discussions with others whether it really *matters* if a person is responsible for their own predicament or need or the degree to which the person might be responsible. Does it really define what *we* are to do as caregivers?

Does it really *matter* if a person is responsible for their own predicament or need or the degree to which the person might be responsible?
Does it really define what *we* are to do as caregivers?

Jesus noted that society is always going to have the poor in its midst (see Matthew 26:11). This is one of the most realistic statements in the entire Bible! No matter how much or how little a person may have—intellectually, materially, physically, spiritually, emotionally—there is always going to be someone who has less (and who is perceived by us as poor) and someone who has more (and, in comparison, we perceive ourselves as poor). Equal starting points never turn out to have equal finish lines. All racers may begin at an agreed-upon starting signal, but not all will complete the race before them in a tie.

Knowing that there are others who are "better off" should produce in us a sense of appreciation and, perhaps, the aspiration to do better, work harder, and rise to a higher plateau. It should produce in us a gracious ability to applaud stellar performance and recognize superior achievement. It must *not* foster jealousy, envy, or resentment.

Knowing that there are others who are "poorer" should produce in us a deep sense of concern, compassionate action, and a genuine willingness to give, help, or serve. It must not produce snobbery or pride.

We each have the possibility of experiencing both ends of the spectrum from rich to poor, in some area of our lives, at some point.

Defining the "Whole" of Poverty

When President Lyndon B. Johnson first announced the War on Poverty in the 1960s, he stated that the goal was to offer a "hand up," not a "hand out." The practical means of waging the war, however, was a massive increase in welfare spending. The American poverty rate was at fifteen percent when the program launched, and it remained at this same level for years. The giving of money alone (and goods and services that were given monetary "value") produced a cycle of dependence, not independence.[1]

What was missing?

Most people who have reflected on this at length have concluded that the missing dimension was personal involvement—those in need were not required to work *alongside* those who could show them the way "up."

It is not only the government, of course, that has tended to throw money at the impoverished rather than to extend human relationships to the poor in a holistic way. The holistic approach addresses the poor in spirit, the poor in education, and the poor who are hungry, homeless, and in need of adequate clothing.

The Poor in Spirit. What does it mean to be poor in spirit? Jesus taught, "Blessed are the poor in spirit, for theirs is the kingdom of heaven" (Matthew 5:3).

It is good to note that Jesus did not begin this statement of "blessing" by saying, "Blessed are the poor financially." Jesus was first and foremost concerned with a spiritual lack.

In a World Bank study titled *Voices of the Poor: Can Anyone Hear Us?*, a woman from Uganda is reported as saying, "When one is poor, she has no say in public, she feels inferior."[2] Other people quoted in this publication point toward other aspects of psychological and sociological poverty.

It is a good exercise for any small group in a church to ask: How do *you* define "poor in spirit"?

Answers might include the following:

- Loneliness and feelings of isolation
- Feelings of low self-worth or low self-esteem
- Feelings of inferiority[3]
- Lack of respect from others, including lack of ability to speak and be heard
- Lack of being recognized—being "invisible" even in a crowded room
- Lack of hope, or pervasive hopelessness and despair
- Lack of love—both of feeling lovable and experiencing affection, even simple acts of touching
- Very few, if any, genuine friends
- Feeling that you are being talked about but never spoken to in a way that is conversational and affirming
- Not being invited to "join in"

Those who give material goods to the poor generally do so in a very structured way, or in a hurry. A family might volunteer to deliver Thanksgiving or Christmas baskets of food or distribute blankets to the homeless and make this an outing—with virtually no expectation of ever seeing again those to whom the gifts are given. When this happens, the "poor folk" become objects more than people. In many cases, the recipients themselves are never asked sincerely and compassionately, "What would you like to receive?" And, sadly, those who give are often disappointed that they do not receive what they perceive to be adequate appreciation for their giving.

Taking the long view of poverty, we all come to the place of acknowledging that *every* person is impoverished in some way. None of us is as rich in spirit as we might be or as rich in spirit as God desires.

Broken Relationships. In *When Helping Hurts*[4], Steve Corbett and Brian Fikkert point out that poverty is rooted in broken relationships—it doesn't exist in a vacuum. It is very helpful to remind volunteers that every person who receives faith-based caregiving has a broken relationship with God, self, other people, or creation in general. When brokenness is acknowledged, it can begin to be healed. People are wounded in relationships—they can be healed through relationships.

As a pastor who works full-time in a church setting, I see tremendous benefit in the role the church can play in alleviating spiritual poverty. Times of prayer, hearing the Word of God preached, participating in Communion, having fellowship with other Christians—these are all sacred activities that can help heal a person who is wounded spiritually.

Most people in material poverty are also impoverished emotionally. For many of these people, having a person available to listen and to be an intentional presence in their lives is of huge benefit.

The first step in addressing poverty is nearly always an act of confession and repentance on the part of the volunteer who seeks to make a difference.[5] This is as simple and profound as a heartfelt prayer: "Lord, I have not loved my neighbor as myself. I am truly sorry and I humbly repent. Please forgive me and use me to love others in a deeper and more effective way—to extend mercy, forgiveness, and acceptance to those to whom You lead me."

Here are ten of the ways I encourage our volunteers to help heal those to whom they volunteer their time, talent, and resources.

1. *Involve the Person in Their Own Development.*[6] Always look for an opportunity to ask individuals to participate in their own development—perhaps to learn something new or to participate in a giving activity even when the person thinks he or she has nothing to offer or give.

   Corbett and Fikkert believe "Participation is not just a means to an end, but rather a legitimate end in its own right."[7] Include others. Participate *with* them.

2. *Focus on the Good.* Focus on the capabilities, skills, and resources of the person—not their lack or problem. In setting goals, make sure they are truly for the good of *all* those directly involved. Continually seek win-win results.

3. *Involve Outside Help if It Is Available.*[8] Bring in outside resources when they are available and appropriate. Don't duplicate what is being provided—but do seek to augment current caregiving efforts.

   At the same time, avoid paternalism. Refuse to do for others what they can do for themselves.[9]

4. *Be Precise in Terminology. Relief* tends to be defined as an urgent and temporary provision of care, often as emergency aid—such as a woman

who needs refuge from physical abuse or a neighborhood that needs help in the wake of a natural catastrophe.[10] *Rehabilitation* is usually an ongoing developmental effort to remedy an existing negative situation. It may take years or decades to fully remedy a situation, often with almost as many steps backward as forward.[11]

In most cases, a person in need of relief must rely on the help of others. Existing resources are depleted. Those who are in a rehabilitation process need encouragement, information, opportunities for skills development, and assistance—but they also must exert some degree of participation and a willingness to change in order for genuine rehabilitation to occur.

5. *Think Holistically.* This means to consider *a totality of need* in a person, family, or community. You may only be able to address one factor or one aspect of need at a time, but it is helpful to have a perspective of the whole and to be open to ways in which related or extended needs might be addressed.

6. *Take an Assets-Based Approach to Development.*[12] A need-based approach focuses on what is wrong. An assets-based approach focuses on available resources, gifts, people, skills, and other positives that might make for beneficial change or transformation.

7. *Walk Alongside.* Do not see yourself as leading the way but rather as walking alongside a person or group. In truth, every volunteer can also use some degree of restoration with God, self, others, and creation. See yourself as on a life journey together with those you serve. Put yourself in a position to receive as well as to give—not necessarily seeking to receive from the very individual or group to whom you give, but to receive nonetheless. God has *His* own ways of giving back to those who give. Always think in terms of interdependence (mutuality of giving and receiving) and partnership (toward mutual goals).

Be willing to share control and leadership—and be the first to applaud and appreciate others. But also be willing to take risks and exert initiative when necessary.

8. *Adopt a Perspective of Growth and Development.* Development and growth are good terms to use when describing or defining the inevitable ongoing changes that occur throughout a person's life and throughout the life of a church, organization, or ministry. Choose to be in a

continual process of assessing, exploring, learning, and adopting. Set goals. Make action plans for pursuing goals.

9. *Assess and Regroup.* Periodically set aside intentional time and effort to reassess goals, priorities, effectiveness, and benefits (including awards and rewards).

10. *Thank and Praise God!* Never stop thanking God for the opportunity to know Jesus Christ, to follow Him, and to serve His purposes! Never stop praising God for His comforting presence and enabling power.

ENDNOTES

1 Robert Rector, "The War on Poverty: 50 years of failure," Heritage Foundation http://www.heritage.org/research/commentary/2014/9/50-years-of-failure-in-the-war-on-poverty. (September 23, 2014).

2 Deepa Narayan with Raj Patel, Kai Schafft, Anne Rademacher, Sarah Kock-Schulte, *Voices of the Poor: Can Anyone Hear Us?* (New York: Oxford Univ. Press for the World Bank, 2000), 65, as quoted in Steve Corbett and Brian Fikkert, *When Helping Hurts: How to Alleviate Poverty without Hurting the Poor ... and Yourself* (Chicago: Moody Press, 2009, 2012), 50.

3 Ibid., 61.

4 Ibid., 58. Adapted from Bryant L. Myers, Walking with the Poor: Principles and Practices of Transformational Development (Mary Knoll, N.Y. Orbis Books, 1999), 27.

5 Ibid., 64.

6 Ibid., 139-140. Adapted from B. de Negri, E. Thomas, A. Illinigumugabo, I. Muvandi, and G. Lewis, Empowering Communities: Participatory Techniques in Community-Based Programme Development. Volume 1 (2): Trainer's Manual (Participant's Handbook) (Nairobi, Kenya: Center for African Family Studies, 1998), 4.

7 Ibid., 136.

8 Ibid., 121.

9 Ibid., 109.

10 Ibid., 104-105.

11 Ibid., 105-106.

12 Ibid., 119-120, 126-127. Assets-based assessment has become widely known through the work of John Kretzmann and John McKnight of the Asset-Based Community Development Institute at Northwestern University.

9

Gaining a New Personal Perspective on the Needy

We live in a fallen world filled with problems. A person doesn't need to look far to find a broken system or a broken life—very often, it means looking in one's own mirror.

The good news of God's Word is that there is a *solution* for all problems. That solution is *more of God*. The Bible tells us from cover to cover that God desires to set things right and that He will give us the wisdom to do our part in His processes.

Very often we seem to think of poverty as being material in nature.[1] It goes far beyond money and possessions. As stated in the previous chapter, poverty is rooted in broken relationships, including a person's relationship with God, with self, with others, and with the rest of creation.[2]

The first step toward alleviating poverty always lies in repentance.[3] We must make a conscious, intentional decision that we are going to turn away from our pride and feeling of superiority and turn toward others. We are called to extend ourselves to others, and the amazing truth is, the more we do this, the more *we* are made whole. If there is one sentence that sums up our call, it is this: "For God so loved the world that He *gave*" (see John 3:16). That is our mission—to turn ourselves outward with love and to give all that we have to the best of our ability to all whom we see in need.

I work in an office that is adjacent to a beautiful cathedral. I am ordained as a clergy person. But in far simpler terms, I am a part of the body of Christ that gathers in this fine old building a few feet from my office door. I am increasingly aware that the church is my practical means for alleviating the poverty in my own life and that I am not alone in this. The prayers, sacraments, preaching of the Word, breaking of bread, and ongoing fellowship with other members of the body are vital to my spiritual life. They are points of very real connection that meet the poverty of my spirit.

The more my spirit is nourished and made whole, the more I am motivated to share this very good news with others. When I experience the gracious gifts of God poured into my life through His Son, Jesus Christ, and by the power of His Holy Spirit, the quicker I am to say to others, "There's life available! Eternal life! Abundant life! A life of wholeness and growth and reward!" I have no doubt whatsoever that those who turn to the fountain of life made available in the church are those who truly become rich in spirit, and this richness spills over into relationships with other people and into a desire to do all that we can both to connect with others and enrich their lives.

The foremost things we give? I contend they are time and presence.

When we make ourselves available to others—spending time listening to their hearts, joining them in their struggles, working alongside them to make a positive difference—we become living vessels of God's hope and love. We truly become the Lord's voice of encouragement, His outstretched arms of compassion, His hands that heal and help, and His feet that are willing to go wherever He calls us to go.

The person who gives time and presence does not do things *for* others as much as *with* others. We must always be on the alert for ways in which to involve the needy in the process of their own growth and development. We must look for their "assets" and build on them.

We must specifically seek to know:

- *Their gifts—including their abilities, information base, and existing skill sets.* We can always be encouraged—every group of people, no matter how poor, uneducated, or underprivileged, has gifts. They know something, can do something, and usually *want* to do what they can do—especially if they are appreciated as individuals with value.[4]

- *Their desires—their dreams and their goals.* Their desires may not be our desires for them. That is sometimes a hard realization for a group of people eager to give and to see rapid progress.

Adopting an Assets-Based Mindset in Our Serving

Assets-Based Mapping is increasingly being utilized to address the needs of the poor—indeed, the needs we find in any body of people, including the local church. The assets of any person and any group include their capabilities, skills, and resources. And this is a threefold approach that is not only effective in helping individuals but in helping entire neighborhoods and communities.[5]

- *Capabilities.* Who has the capacity to do? To give? To receive? Open minds and open hearts always create an open door for ministry!

- *Skills.* What specific skills are required to meet a specific need? Who has those skills? Who can be taught the ongoing skills necessary for maintenance, growth, and ongoing expansion?

- *Resources.* Most needs require something that is tangible—it may be a book from which to read or a slate and a piece of chalk with which to write (or pencil and paper, or an electronic tablet). It may be a teacher on tape or videotape, or a mentoring adult sitting close by. Meeting a need takes people and money—but never money alone. The best solutions and answers involve money that can be planted into *means and methods* that inspire participation by the needy in the working out of their own future.

In the vast majority of cases, we have found that the resources are already within the needy person or needy neighborhood to *some degree.* The process is not one of providing nearly as much as it is of tapping into and bringing forth the talents, skills, and desires that are already embedded deep within.

A Change in Perspective

Many people find they feel challenged to adopt a new perspective on the poor the more they work *with* them. They often feel compelled:

- To move from a need-based perspective to an assets-based focus. A need-based perspective puts emphasis on what is wrong; assets-based focus looks at the resources available (gifts, talents, resources). A need-based focus is usually task-oriented and short-term. An assets-based perspective tends to be relationship-building and long-term, even to the point of seeking eternal change.

- To develop goals and plans that require participation by the recipients of caregiving and include definitions for responsibility and accountability.

- To engage those they serve in activities that promote reciprocity, mutual prayer, and mentoring.

- To begin a process that involves an ongoing assessment of needs, learning of skills, emphasis on character development, and establishment of interim goals (and plans for reaching them).

- To become aware of the need for *healthy* relationships between givers and receivers and of unhealthy relationships. Not all mentoring situations are good; not all "partnering" relationships are healthy. Standards generally need to be set, including mutual input into what the standards might be and periodic evaluation as to whether the standards are being kept.

Addressing the Issue of Entitlement

We live in a time when the word *entitlement* is used in both directions—those who are impoverished feel entitled to have someone care and respond to their neediness, and those who are in a position to give often resent those who *expect* all of their needs to be met. Surely we must come to a middle ground.

Entitled. We are *all* entitled to:

- Expressions of God's love—*through* God's people
- Respect for our personhood and expressions of value that we are beloved children of God
- Opportunities to work, to vote, to give voice to opinions, to gather socially, to worship God, to *pursue* our dreams and hopes
- Believe in God and to trust God to forgive us and help us

Not Entitled. Conversely, *none* of us is entitled to:

- Require another person to take on total responsibility for meeting our basic needs (except, perhaps, those who are severely mentally or physically disabled to the point that they cannot contribute anything toward their own sustenance)
- A life of willful laziness or greed
- Commit crimes against other people or ourselves

When we look at what Jesus says we are entitled to as God's beloved creation and compare it with what we often think we are entitled to, we are likely to find significant gaps and differences!

Avoiding Toxic Charity

The term *toxic charity* has been used by urban activist Robert Lupton to describe benevolent activities that may be well intentioned but can actually do more harm than good.[6]

We are wise to adopt the first rule of good medical care, which is presented as the primary and foremost principle to those who are in training to become physicians and nurses: *do no harm.*

Our desire, of course, is to do good, and even great good. But by all means, we must be aware that the potential is always there for us to do harm, even great harm, if we are not aware of what we are doing.

Refuse to Settle for a Quick Fix

We tend to expect rehabilitation and development to be fast-moving processes. They are not. We may be able to give a degree of relief—which is often described as a temporary provision of aid, often with a sense of urgency or in an emergency crisis. But genuine development and rehabilitation are *processes* that require ongoing effort, time, and resources.

This is not at all to say that nothing should be done unless it can be done over the long haul. There are situations when short-term relief efforts are vital for the continuation of life or health. It is to say that we must be mindful that in *most* cases, change and growth take time and a hefty dose of perseverance and patience. We must be diligent in our efforts and persistent in our prayers.

Rejecting Tendencies to Be Paternalistic

Paternalism is doing things for people that they can do for themselves.[7] None of us is called to "parent" the poor; we are not required to take on that responsibility, nor are we given the authority by God to take on that role. We *are* called to befriend, to help, and to walk a journey of faith *with* others who are willing to walk with us.

In like manner, we must reject all tendencies to become co-dependent with those around us. The needy must not depend on us solely and insistently for their needs to be met. We must not depend on *their* need of us to give us our identity or sense of self-worth.

There is a healthy balance to be achieved in caregiving relationships. We must seek it until we find it!

Staying Alert for Barrier Removal

We must not lose sight of the social justice dimension of the Good Samaritan parable.

This is a story about breaking down barriers—racial, economic, social, cultural, and religious. The Samaritans were of a different racial mix than the Jews. They lived in a designated region of the land. They had their own temple and religious services. They had few economic or social ties with the larger Jewish population. Jesus challenged this norm. We must do the same.

A number of years ago, I volunteered at a soup kitchen. A woman came in and sat down across the aisle from me. She was dirty and unkempt. Her body odor was strong, and she had only a few teeth.

I justified to myself all sorts of reasons why I did not need to engage this woman in conversation, but then I heard the Spirit of the Lord speak deep within my spirit: "Connie, will you hug her?"

Such a simple question. There should have been no delay in my response, but there was.

Yes, I went to her, and yes, I asked her if I could give her a hug. She was as surprised at my asking as I was! I gave her a little hug and received a big smile in return.

It was a little thing.

Or was it?

How can we ever tell how the Lord sees our obedience or what He might do when we obey?

Examine Your Own Motives

I once heard a story about a young woman who had gone on a band trip to participate in a parade in a nearby community. The band members were encouraged to bring along five dollars so they could buy their lunch after the parade and maybe do a small amount of shopping in the town before the bus ride back to their own community.

This woman said that she and two of her friends met a band member from another town as they stored their instruments, hats, and uniform jackets and headed for lunch. The new girl didn't have money for lunch, so the three girls who did have money paid for her hamburger and shared their French fries. Over lunch, the girl told them a little about her life—her dad had been sent to prison and her mother was trying to pay the bills, and the girl herself said she was trying to get a job but finding it difficult since she was two months too young to get a work permit. The three band friends felt sorrow for the girl's condition welling up in them. By the time lunch was over, they had a little huddle and mutually agreed to give the girl all of the change they still had from their lunch money. They handed over almost ten dollars to this new friend. (Hamburgers and French fries were cheaper in those days!)

Later, a person who knew this girl said to them, "You were scammed. She was fishing for cigarette money."

The three girls were stunned and a little embarrassed that they had been so naïve, but then, one of the girls said, "Just because her heart wasn't right doesn't mean that our hearts weren't right."

What a great attitude! What a great approach to helping.

Even if a needy person doesn't respond in the way a caregiver might desire, there's no cause to stop caring. We must never stop reaching out. It is not our place to determine or even to *know* how a care-receiver responds. That's the work of the Holy Spirit—and we must trust Him to do what only He can do. Our role is to give in the ways He leads us to give.

Consider Intentionally Taking the Oath for Compassionate Service

Robert Lupton is the founder of Family Consultation Services, which has recently been renamed Focused Community Strategies, in Atlanta, Georgia. I highly endorse his Oath for Compassionate Service[8] which is paraphrased here.

1. I will never do for others what they have (or could have) the capacity to do for themselves.

2. I will limit my one-way giving to emergency situations and seek always to find ways and means for legitimate exchange.

3. I will seek ways to empower the poor through hiring, lending, and investing and use grants sparingly as incentives that reinforce achievements.

4. I will put the interests of the poor above my own (or organizational) self-interest even when it may be costly.

5. I will take time to listen and carefully assess both expressed and unspoken needs so that my actions will ultimately strengthen rather than weaken the hands of those I would serve.

6. Above all, to the best of my ability, I will do no harm.

Three excellent resources on this general topic are:
- *When Helping Hurts* by Steve Corbett and Brian Fikkert
- *Toxic Charity* by Robert Lupton
- *Charity Detox* by Robert Lupton

ENDNOTES

1   Steve Corbett and Brian Fikkert, *When Helping Hurts: How to Alleviate Poverty without Hurting the Poor ... and Yourself* (Chicago: Moody Press, 2009, 2012), 52-53.

2   Ibid., 54-59.

3   Ibid., 64.

4   Ibid., 120.

5   Ibid., 119-120, 126-127.

6   Robert Lupton, *Toxic Charity* (New York: HarperCollins Publishers, 2012).

7   Steve Corbett and Brian Fikkert, *When Helping Hurts*, 109.

8   Adapted from *Toxic Charity* by Robert Lupton (New York: HarperCollins Publishers, 2012) 8-9, 128-132.

10

Developing a Corridor

For the past few years, we have made efforts to expand our work at Eugene Field Elementary School to create a natural extension of mentoring to the local junior high school, Clinton Middle School, which is where many of the Eugene Field graduates go, and ultimately to the nearby high school, Webster High School. It seemed no accident to us that the junior high and high school were just down the boulevard, so to speak, from Eugene Field. We began to refer to this area as our Local Field, the West Tulsa Corridor.

Recognizing Changes in Ministry Methods

When we began our community outreach to Eugene Field Elementary School more than twenty years ago, there was no concept for terms that are mainstream in our culture today: tweeting, status updates, emails, Skyping, or texting.

We have been very focused at First United Methodist in our desire to be a mission-minded church and to be aware that methodology has and will continue to change and that we are wise to embrace these changes and use them for outreach. One of the conclusions we have drawn in recent years is that our foreign missionaries are, in many ways, no more distant than our local volunteer ministers who are working in neighborhood and school locations.

In late 2012, First United Methodist Director of Global Outreach, Kelly Junk, led the way as our church identified three strategic focus areas for ministry:
- *The Local Field*—West Tulsa Corridor. In 2013, First United Methodist hired Shelli Pleasant as the Local Field Coordinator.
- *The Near Field*—Guatemala
- *The Far Field*—North Africa

The designation of these three mission fields was not in any way designed to diminish concern for a particular missionary or mission but rather to help *local* volunteers to see themselves as missionaries and to see the great connection between what is done in the Local Field and the Near and Far Fields. In all, First

United Methodist supports seventeen Faith Promise missionaries throughout the world with a deep commitment to loving and caring for each of them.

The church leadership adopted a threefold goal:

One: engage the entire congregation, all ages, in these three mission fields.

Two: seek to impact a community and, over time, a village, city, and nation for Christ.

Three: leave a "holy footprint," a legacy, that in years to come, the congregation and God might say, "Well done, good and faithful servants."

This goal orientation led to active searching for ways that *every* mission or service activity might grow and have greater influence in an organic way. We sought to trust the Holy Spirit to lead us to areas adjacent to our current work that *He* was opening up and, at the same time, to speak to individuals who might become champions or volunteers for a particular ministry.

Organizationally, we formed a Local Field team to blend the activities, prayer focus, and goal-setting for two departments in the church that had been distinct: missions (foreign) and community ministries. Kelly and I saw it as no accident that we had been personal friends for more than fifty years! We were on the same page in our desire for greater missional activity in all of our volunteer ministries.

We set as our first priority the bridging of the gap between our church and the communities in which we volunteer.

An Ordered Expansion

The concept of the West Tulsa Corridor provides opportunities for the expansion of ministry in three dimensions:

- Spatial expansion

- Organization or networking expansion, with more partnering relationships possible

- Generational expansion, an opportunity to recruit future volunteers as children from Eugene Field eventually graduate from high school and bring a new level of compassion and prosperity back to their neighborhoods

That is the perceived potential and goal.

Our question became, "How might these mainstay ministry outreaches at Eugene Field *expand* to Clinton Middle School and Webster High School?"

We were aware that a number of former Eugene Field students who had benefited from our mentoring programs and other activity and reward programs were at these schools—but we had made no specific plan to follow Eugene Field students to Clinton or Webster.

We began to make a concerted effort to find examples in our own church of people who had been involved in the West Tulsa Corridor even before we gave it a name. Indeed, *some* contact had been maintained by individual mentors and their mentees. And much of that contact seemed to focus on the Wyldlife program we began at Clinton Middle School but did not have enough traction to continue.

Wyldlife is a middle school outreach of an organization called Young Life. Its mission is to "model and express God's love to our young friends by learning their names, hearing their stories, and honoring their God-given desire for a life of fun, adventure, and purpose." That mission statement certainly fit our purposes at First United Methodist.

In December 2011, we focused our Christmas offering on two projects, one of which was Clinton Middle School. First United Methodist Church has a long-standing heritage of generous Christmas giving, and it seemed a natural extension of our care to help with projects in the Clinton Middle School community, especially the Wyldlife program and Rebuilding Together Tulsa, an organization that brings volunteers and communities together to improve the homes and lives of low-income homeowners. The donation that year was $23,000, and it went a long way toward restoring physical homes and providing a safe place and safe relationships for teenagers in need.

The church did not just throw money at Clinton. For a number of Saturdays throughout 2012, First United Methodist members could be found replacing windows, repairing roofs, laying floors, gardening, and painting homes in the Clinton neighborhood. When people asked, "Why are you doing this?" church members took it as their cue to tell about Jesus. A number of families who opened their homes for repair eventually opened their lives to Christ's love.

For three years, we also paid the registration fee for a number of Clinton students to attend Wyldlife Camp in Michigan and Texas.

A New Master Plan for the Eugene Field Area

Growing Together is a community partnership established in 2011 to connect organizations, residents, and educators to enable children to live, learn, and thrive in their neighborhoods and schools. The partnership was incubated by Community Action Project Tulsa.

Very specifically, the plan calls for three "pillars" to be put into place to help break a cycle of poverty in a targeted neighborhood:

- Quality education (Pre-K to 12)
- Quality mixed-income housing
- Community vibrancy (safe streets and parks, quality amenities, etc., especially a library and transportation)

The Eugene Field neighborhood was one of the targeted areas, and we quickly became a part of this collaborative effort. We were glad to see that the funding was a true blend of private and government sources. The HUD and Department of Education funds were only for planning; implementation has been funded mostly by the Schustermann and George Kaiser Family Foundations and the Tulsa Area United Way. We were also very pleased to see that the overall goals of the partnership were very much in line with the goals we have had for two decades.

Throughout our decades of community ministries, First United Methodist Church has held to the strong opinion that *collaboration is key*. Collaboration is a mindset that means we seek to work *with* people rather than *for* people. We have sought to make every endeavor a win-win opportunity, with the people in the community or school having an equal voice in all decision-making and methods. Relationship is not only at the heart of neighbor-to-neighbor activities—relationship *is* the activity!

Relationship is not only at the heart of neighbor-to-neighbor activities—relationship *is* the activity.

The true heart of collaboration is a ministry of reconciliation, which must always be conducted with an attitude of humility and without a fixed agenda, timetable, or goals that might be more man-made than Spirit-led.

A wonderful example of collaboration has taken root at Eugene Field in the last couple of years. It is an affiliation that we have heartily embraced. Growing Together brought Reading Partners to Eugene Field.

Reading Partners is a national organization that has been shown to be highly effective in helping children improve their reading skills. In a national study published in 2014, students in the Reading Partners program were compared to students in a control group, and the Reading Partners program was found to have a statistically significant impact on reading comprehension, reading fluency, and sight-word reading—the three most common measures of student reading proficiency.

The Reading Partners program was shown to be effective for a variety of students—both male and female, non-native English speakers as well as native English speakers, and students from different grades or baseline reading achievement levels.

This program has been watched closely in Oklahoma, which has instituted state laws requiring third-graders to display reading skills before they are promoted to fourth grade. While lip service had been given to reading ability in years past, the new rulings were enforced in 2014, and hundreds of students across our city (and hundreds more across the state) were informed that they would *not* be advanced to the fourth grade unless they participated in summer school tutorials on reading or provided other documentation indicating that they could read at the level required.

To our joy, every student at Eugene Field but one demonstrated reading proficiency. In other words, the vast majority of Eugene Field third-graders were performing on par with the state's standards.

Oklahoma is by no means the only state with reading deficiency at the elementary school level. A study reported by MDRC, a nonprofit, nonpartisan education and social policy research firm, found that nationwide, two out of three fourth-graders were reading below grade level and almost one-third of children lacked even basic reading skills. It has been well documented, of course, that children who struggle with reading in elementary school are at high risk of academic failure, high school dropout, and other negative outcomes.

In many ways, Reading Partners is very similar to the reading program in which we at First United Methodist first participated more than two decades ago. The schools that have shown the greatest benefit from Reading Partners have been those with volunteers who have been very faithful in their volunteer work.

We have been very pleased to collaborate with Reading Partners.

The Future

What do collaborative efforts such as the Growing Together community partnership and Reading Partners mean for us at First United Methodist Church?

First, we do not see our involvement in community ministries as lessening. If we have learned one thing in the past twenty years, it is that new opportunities for growth and development in the community mean new opportunities for us to serve. We believe our role as volunteers may change *to a degree* but that we will find *increased* rather than decreased areas in which we can and will serve.

Second, we regard affiliations with other groups as giving us new groups of people to reach with the gospel. Relationships offer excellent ground for evangelism, and working together with others is an excellent way to share values and faith.

Relationships offer excellent ground for evangelism, and working together with others is an excellent way to share values and faith.

Third, we realize that with growing opportunity, we will need more efficient ways of ministering to others. One way to become more efficient and effective is to deploy volunteers in more intentional ways to experience collective impact. We will also need more volunteers. There likely will never be a lessening of need on any front in which we are currently involved as a church. Rather, there will be a need for more workers to help with the harvest.

We continue to maintain that the school is a hub for any neighborhood or community—it is a prime place for evangelism, ministry, and for taking on the challenge of defeating poverty. We also continue to regard our church volunteer efforts as creating a bridge across which students, parents, and neighbors can walk freely—all the way to a relationship with Jesus Christ.

11

Establishing an Anchorhold

Several years ago First United Method Church began to dream and pray about a ministry that we call "Anchorhold." A small group of us met every Monday for a year to discern the specifics related to the direction we felt the Lord was leading us to take.

Overall, our vision for this ministry was well-defined and extremely organic—in other words, we expected it to develop in natural human ways according to factors in the immediate environment in which an Anchorhold house or community might be established.

To understand what Anchorhold is, it may be helpful to begin with what it is *not*:

Anchorhold is *not* a church-based program. In other words, people do not go to church in order to take part in an Anchorhold group or to attend Anchorhold meetings. Anchorhold is rooted in a neighborhood, and it is intended to be a neighbor-to-neighbor, Christ-centered example of a "way to live." It is not a *program* as much as it is a *living pattern*.

Residency is open to adults of all ages who are either a post-secondary school student or are employed in an outside job. Residents are sought who have experience in prayer, hospitality, evangelism, and social justice work and who, most of all, are willing to let the Lord lead them to be *His* hands and feet as they relate to the neighbors around them.

Both young and old and people of varying races and cultural backgrounds are welcome in an Anchorhold residence or community.

Anchorhold residents volunteer to live in an Anchorhold community for one year. If, after that year, the person or couple decides that they might like to extend their stay, the Anchorhold ministry leadership and the residents meet for a season of prayer and discernment before a decision to extend the stay is reached. No person or couple is expected to become a resident of Anchorhold permanently. Rather, the Anchorhold experience is perceived to be a step deeper in a person's or couple's life toward an ongoing life of intentionality in outreach within a neighborhood.

The Anchorhold concept has roots in Perkins Seminary in Dallas and The Upper Room in Nashville. The idea was birthed in an extended conversation and prayer between evangelism professor and pastor Elaine Heath and several of her students at Perkins. Concurrently, in another part of the nation, Reverend Tom Albin was developing the concept of "mission-evangelists" who might live together for a year in communities around the world where God's light was dim. These two streams of ministry focus came together to become a missions opportunity called "Missions Year." Anchorhold has taken that a step further, reaching into local neighborhoods.

A New Type of Community

Anchorhold has four major facets: prayer, hospitality, work, and outreach— all on a disciplined daily and weekly schedule.

Some have described it as a new way of living in community that is very similar to lay monastic communities through the centuries, especially in Europe. If there is a philosophical champion for the Anchorhold concept, it would be Dietrich Bonhoeffer. Bonhoeffer, author of *Life Together*, wrote in a letter to his brother dated January 14, 1935, saying "The restoration of the church will surely come only from a new type of monasticism which has nothing in common with the old but a complete lack of compromise in a life lived in accordance with the Sermon on the Mount in the discipleship of Christ."

By definition, an anchorhold is the grip of an anchor, a firm hold, a synonym for security. Another definition of anchorhold comes from the monastics. It was an intentional place where those who had taken vows to become cloistered could meet with persons from the outside community to offer spiritual guidance and provide food for the poor. For us at First United Methodist, it is the prayerful residence of persons who have chosen to draw apart from culture at large to unite their lives for spiritual purposes.

Anchorhold, in our experience as a church, is a concept that can be applied to a residence—a house or small apartment complex. It can also refer to a group of houses in close proximity within a neighborhood. The community is formed around a geographical center, with participating residents deciding that they will share their lives in a way that creates a "micro-community."

What ties Anchorhold residents and residences together are these life-style-related commitments, termed a Rule of Life:

- *A commitment to servant leadership*—with members sharing life with their non-Anchorhold neighbors in order to model the gospel to them and influence them for a renewed or deeper relationship with Jesus Christ.

- *A commitment to a monastic Rule of Life*—with members sharing a daily discipline of prayer, reading, and study of the Scriptures and an intentional desire to listen better to God and others in order to become more faithful witnesses for Christ in our world today.

The residents of our Anchorhold house are members of First United Methodist Church. The rules of covenant that order the houses are rules of life, which are seen as an extension of the covenant commitment a person makes at the time he or she becomes a member at First Methodist—prayer, presence, gifts, service, and witness.

Some have called the Anchorhold lifestyle "contemplative living." One of the Anchorhold house residents describes the discipline as "living the Christian life out loud."

In summary, the residents of the Anchorhold house follow a rhythm of disciplined prayer and Bible study, shared meals, and volunteer service. They *consciously* and *intentionally* seek to connect with their neighbors, and in so doing, to become witnesses to their life in Christ Jesus. The goal is to develop *Christ-centered relationships* with others in a community that is largely unchurched.

First United Methodist Church continues to be in the organic stages of establishing an Anchorhold community in west Tulsa in our Local Field. We have also offered a similar mission-year internship in North Africa.

Why do this? Those who conceived and birthed the Anchorhold concept at First United Methodist did so with three main motivations:

- First, a strong conclusion from Scripture that people are supposed to grow spiritually in community, not isolation.

- Second, a conclusion that the most effective Christian communities are those that are Spirit-led, with the understanding that the Spirit leads through a witness to two or more people who are in full reconciliation and fellowship with God and with one another.

- Third, a conviction that genuine Christians are intended to develop relationships with non-Christian neighbors, trusting God to lead their conversations and neighborly ties without a set formula or top-down church management, all of which can be "messy" at times.

Words that occur frequently in discussions about Anchorhold and in conversations with Anchorhold residents are *transformational* and *transformative*. Those who seem drawn to an Anchorhold commitment believe strongly that a relationship with Jesus includes a mandate for living in a constant state of renewal or spiritual growth. That ultimately involves a transformation from a *former* way of living and thinking to a *new* way of living, thinking, and of interacting with others.

Even so, those who have signed on to Anchorhold affiliations are convinced that:

- Many neighborhoods have been abandoned—they have no evangelistic outreach from churches that may even be located within their neighborhood.

- The poor and the needy tend to be overlooked and under-welcomed by churches.

- Racial and economic divides can and must be healed.

- People pray with greater faith and greater faithfulness the more they pray together.

- The world as a whole needs many more "embassies" of reconciliation—places where those who do not know Christ Jesus can see a Christ-centered, Spirit-led life modeled for them and learn how to become and then be followers of the Lord Jesus.

The goals are lofty, indeed. But the lifestyle in these homes and neighborhoods is very practical. Members meet together for prayer and Scripture study. They routinely eat meals together and enjoy recreational times together (which may be tending a large garden or exercising). They host dinner parties for their neighbors. They actively reach out to their neighbors with a genuine desire to get to know them. They are open at all times to ways in which the Spirit might direct their relationships and activities, but they are not pushy in their attitude or demeanor.

Those who express an interest in being part of Anchorhold are challenged to find where Jesus is already transforming a neighborhood and then join Him there.

Dropping Anchor in a Westside Community

Let me quickly note that our first Anchorhold house in Tulsa was *not* directly connected to Eugene Field Elementary School or the immediate neighborhood. The house, nonetheless, is located just a few miles from the school.

Our first Anchorhold house was chosen for three main reasons. First, it was located close to an existing United Methodist church with which we have had affiliation in the past—Epworth United Methodist Church. The house served as the parsonage for the church in years past, but it had not been used for more than a decade in that capacity and was in need of repairs and upgrades.

Second, the house was within the West Tulsa Corridor, our Local Field for missions.

Third, the house was large enough to accommodate three single people or one married couple.

Prayer Walks. We began considering this type of community outreach by conducting a weekly prayer walk. Director of Global Outreach Kelly Junk led the effort. A small group of church members began walking with her weekly. Kelly has said, "We didn't have any agenda—just circling things in prayer."

It was on a prayer walk that future Anchorhold residents met a young man who was preparing to move to Washington, D.C., the next day. He and his father came looking for our church members. He said, "I have been walking this neighborhood in prayer, too! I have asked the Lord, 'Who will take up the mantle?' And then we met you on an early, cold morning." This young man essentially passed the torch of prayer to us!

After a year of walking and listening to the Spirit, the group felt led to pursue a housing option in the Carbondale neighborhood of west Tulsa. Kathy Chenoweth and Sandra Goodson were walking and circling the neighborhood and Epworth United Methodist Church when the pastor of Epworth UMC showed up to find out what the two women were doing. The pastor had received a call telling him that two women were walking on his property. He soon learned the mission of these women, and they, in turn, learned that he was the pastor of the Epworth church. A great friendship was birthed.

Members of Epworth United Methodist Church were invited to participate in the prayer walks. The Epworth congregation, which had an average age of about seventy-five at the time, was eager to see young people and new life on its nine-acre campus, and they were delighted when efforts moved ahead to renovate the unused parsonage.

The house had not been occupied for some time and was not needed as a parsonage. The house was in need of extensive repair, but it seemed ideal to both Epworth and First United Methodist as a place that could become a focal point for intentional ministry and outreach to the general Epworth community.

The renovation of the residence was a true collaborative effort. Gordon Murray and Brad Burkhalter from First United Methodist led the renovation effort, but in all, more than seventy volunteers assisted with the project, including students from Metro Christian Academy in Tulsa, out-of-state volunteers, and dozens of church members from both Epworth and First United Methodist.

The house was ready for occupancy at the very time John and Shelli Pleasant, our champions for this ministry, were ready to move in.

Champions Prepared for the Challenge

John and Shelli Pleasant were members of First United Methodist when they married in 2007. At the time, Shelli was recovering from cancer-related treatments and surgery and was working as the children's department director at the church. John was in the process of shutting down two non-church ministries he had founded, Mountaineers for Christ and Mountain School Teen Adventures.

The Pleasants moved from Tulsa to Phoenix, in part seeking a more simple life, with both of them open to what God might have for them next.

John took a job as a parking lot attendant in Phoenix, not at all a place where he expected anything other than a mindless work routine that might provide the bare minimum for a simple lifestyle in Phoenix. They moved into a neighborhood that had green grass and big trees—not the norm for the desert climate of Phoenix, which often has 130° F temperatures in the summer.

And then two things happened. First, John faced difficulties on the job from a coworker who openly voiced his hatred for Christians. He seemed to say things just to antagonize John. John said, "I had to pray daily just to be able to work with him." Over the months, John challenged the coworker's skepticism with truth, always in private and after praying for wisdom and an ability to speak gently. It wasn't until John resigned from the parking lot position that the young man told him, "You have changed my view of Christianity forever." It was welcome news to John!

A second thing happened in their neighborhood. A thirteen-year-old boy was gunned down about half a block from their home. John and Shelli had heard the shots but were stunned at the outcome. Their near disbelief—"How could this happen *here*?"—turned into intense prayer and action. They began to walk their neighborhood, intentionally getting to know their neighbors and praying for them. They asked God to fill vacant houses with responsible, caring people. They spoke to every neighbor they encountered with a smile. Eventually, they made a pact with their neighbors that any time a neighbor saw an unfamiliar car pull into the neighborhood—people they suspected may be drug purchasers or dealers—they would go outside with their children and dogs and begin talking to other neighbors who did the same. Soon, the unfamiliar cars stopped coming and the neighborhood began having block parties.

A few doors from the Pleasants was a house that had been established for use by transgendered persons. Shelli began saying hello to some of the residents as she encountered them on her prayer walks. They seemed hungry for simple friendship, and John and Shelli felt they were being asked by the Lord to pray for them, love them, and be good neighbors. John said, "And that, we could do!"

After three years in Phoenix, John and Shelli began to pray about two things: one, being more intentional in their commitment to love their neighbors, and two, the possibility of moving back to Tulsa to be nearer to family members. Two weeks after they began these prayers, they received an unexpected financial gift that made a move to Tulsa possible, and they also had a call from a close friend at the church, Kelly Junk, asking them to join her in praying with Reverend Tom Hoffmann about moving into First United Methodist's first Anchorhold house.

Kelly had been telling her friends Shelli and John about the founding of the Anchorhold ministry for about a year, but without any expectation that they might be future residents.

Looking back, both John and Shelli began to see how God had been preparing them for this particular living arrangement and ministry. And during the year, a residence had actually been located and remodeled. It was the God-defined intersection of two roads.

They moved into the Anchorhold house in June of 2013.

The Opportunity for Volunteers

First United Methodist volunteers who do not live in an Anchorhold residence or community are still invited to participate in the ministry in a number of ways:

- *The Garden.* When John and Shelli lived in Phoenix, they were surprised and pleased one day to find neighbors at their door with an armload of homegrown vegetables. They realized that a garden was likely to be an instant relationship-builder in just about any neighborhood. Shortly after they moved into the Anchorhold house, they began to revitalize the raised garden beds that had been built behind the Epworth residence. Volunteers from First United Methodist assisted in planting, weeding, watering, and harvesting from the garden. The food has not only been used by the occupants of Anchorhold but also as love gifts to neighbors.

- *Surveying.* Church volunteers have knocked on doors with questionnaires to discover the talents, gifts, desires, and needs of the people in the neighborhood. John and Shelli Pleasant are not among those who go door-to-door, but they do meet with the volunteers to learn the results of the questionnaires. This approach allows the Pleasants to be simply good caring neighbors without any perception by their neighbors that they may have any ulterior motives.

- *Joining In.* Volunteers from First United Methodist frequently participate in the regular Bible studies and neighborhood meals that the Anchorhold residents host.

- *Prayer.* A number of people join John and Shelli from time to time to walk through the Epworth neighborhood. These volunteers have discovered new insights into what it means to engage in a neighborhood prayer walk and have expressed a new level of desire to walk their *own* neighborhoods and pray. What do the volunteers pray for? We encourage them to pray for:

  1. The physical health of every person who lives in each house
  2. The work—career activities, jobs, companies—of the money-earners in each house, including prayer for ongoing employment and financial stability
  3. The spiritual needs of each person in the house
  4. The emotional health of each person—praying *against* abuse, fear, loneliness, feelings of hopelessness, and sorrow that comes from loss of any kind (death, loss of job, a child moving out of state)
  5. The church or faith community to which the members of the house might belong

If those praying sense that nobody in the household attends church, we ask them to pray that the Holy Spirit will give them an opportunity to invite the family to come to church with them.

Granted, a person isn't likely to be able to cover all five of these areas in the time it will take the person to walk past the front of one house. Some prayer walkers choose to focus on just one of these five areas of need during a particular walk.

Whenever possible, those who go on prayer walks do so with a friend who will join in the prayers.

We encourage all who go on prayer walks to thank God for their neighbors and to praise Him for His ongoing love, mercy, and forgiveness, which is freely extended to every person in the neighborhood. These principles of prayer, of course, are good for *any* person walking his or her neighborhood with a goal of praying.

In an ongoing way, those who move into an Anchorhold house regard prayer as their number one activity and responsibility. Tom Hoffmann told a reporter, "[Our purpose] is not a church plant. We don't assume what the good and right thing to do is. We become God's people in the neighborhood. We are not there to fix the residents of the neighborhood, but rather, we ask the Lord to fix us."

While the idea of Anchorhold may mirror ancient monasteries that had similar houses for those seeking a daily rule of life, in our modern Anchorhold house, none of the residents wear monastic robes, and no set times for prayer services are held in the house. Rather, the residents live together in a disciplined, accountable community, praying daily for themselves and others in their immediate neighborhood to experience more of the presence of Christ. The residents work, pay rent, and seek to support one another in prayer linked to daily Bible study and spiritual disciplines or rhythms.

The residents are always looking for ways to be good neighbors. They recently planted a community garden in which neighborhood children can learn basic principles of gardening and take home a portion of the produce to their families. The residents have had opportunity to share tools with their neighbors and to assist in simple fix-it chores. They have also had several dinner parties with neighbors. In the fall of 2015, they worked with Epworth United Methodist Church during fall break to conduct a three-day vacation church school, teaching Bible stories and songs to the neighborhood children who attended.

We are hopeful that additional Anchorhold houses might take root in other neighborhoods across our city, but at present, we are still very much in the prayer walk stage of developing an understanding about where the Holy Spirit might want us to take root.

The four major ways described above for including non-residential volunteers (in the garden, surveying, Bible studies, and prayer) are of great assistance to the residents, but we are also finding that some of those who volunteer in these ways are being led by the Holy Spirit to want to become residents at an Anchorhold house or to make their home as part of an Anchorhold community.

For more information about Anchorhold-style residences and communities, I recommend:
Missional, Monastic, Mainline by Elaine Heath and Larry Duggins.

12

Ministry to the Volunteers

In many ways, my role as minister of community ministries has truly been a pastoral role—I consider myself to be a minister to the lay ministers who are engaged in our outreach ministries.

Through the years, some of our initial volunteers at Eugene Field struggled with the trauma of beginning a relationship with a child only to have the child move away, often suddenly, without a warning or a goodbye. Others felt sadness that they weren't able to do more to help a child they had grown to love. Still others felt emotionally overwhelmed by the trauma they saw in the children's lives.

In all cases, we had a ministry *within the church* of helping our volunteers to volunteer. There was a major opportunity to teach caring people *how* to love and how to trust God to do *His* work, believing it would far exceed *our* efforts.

Part of my role has been administrative, but the greater percentage of my effort has been directed toward encouraging members to volunteer and to stay involved.

Encouraging People to Volunteer

I am convinced that I have heard all the excuses a person can possibly come up with for choosing not to take on a volunteer ministry role. I have tried to stay lighthearted about excuses and not take them personally.

Without a doubt, excuses abound in our world. They are everywhere. Some people have become self-proclaimed experts in explaining why they did or did not do something or why they can't or we can't either.

As far as I am concerned, we *must* confront our excuses, and this confrontation usually begins in a person's own mirror or in one's own prayer times.

Certainly, excuses are not limited to our modern age. Nobody has *ever* had enough time, resources, ability, or desire to volunteer in ministry. One of the most famous Bible heroes had an excuse mindset. God used him anyway.

Three Excuses God Didn't Accept

We read in Judges 6 about a man named Gideon who had a profound encounter with the Lord. At the time, Gideon and the Israelites were under severe attack by the Midianites, who periodically raided the land and took all the Israelite produce for themselves. Gideon is threshing wheat in a winepress in order to hide it from the Midianites when the Angel of the Lord appears to him, saying, "The Lord is with you, you mighty man of valor!" (Judges 6:12). The Lord further says to him, "Go in this might of yours, and you shall save Israel from the hand of the Midianites." Gideon responds with three major excuses:

EXCUSE #1: I'm not qualified to do this.

Gideon points out that his clan is the weakest in his tribe and that he is the least in his father's house. He does not consider himself at all qualified to pursue or succeed in the task the Lord is describing to him.

God replies, "Surely I will be with you, and you shall defeat the Midianites." (Judges 6:16)

EXCUSE #2: I'm not sure You are calling me to do this.

Gideon asks for a sign, and the Lord directs him to prepare an offering of meat and unleavened bread, pour broth over it, and put it on a rock in a specified place. Gideon does this. When the Angel of the Lord touches the offering with the tip of his staff, fire rises out of the rock and consumes the sacrifice, and the Angel disappears.

Gideon perceives that the Angel was indeed from God and that he meant what he had said.

EXCUSE #3: I'm afraid.

Gideon tries a third excuse: "Alas, O Lord God! For I have seen the Angel of the Lord face to face" (Judges 6:22). This is a statement of fear since Gideon believes fully that a person who sees God is doomed to die. The Lord replies, "Peace be with you; do not fear, you shall not die" (Judges 6:23).

The Lord proceeds to protect Gideon as He commands him to tear down an altar built to the false god Baal. He shows Gideon His power by causing a fleece to remain dry while the ground around it becomes wet, and then for the fleece to be wet while the ground remains dry. The story continues with God causing a large number of men to join Gideon to fight against the Midianites.

Through the years, I have encountered dozens of people who have conveyed to me that they do not feel qualified to do volunteer work, that they aren't sure God wants *their* service, or that they are afraid, usually of failure.

The truth is that *every* person is qualified to be a volunteer. Volunteers come in many shapes and sizes and are suited for a wide variety of serving roles.

The truth is that *God* desires every follower of Jesus Christ to be a willing caregiver to others in need.

The truth is that God is *with* those who volunteer, and He equips them with both courage and skill to do specific tasks and to persevere in them until good results are produced.

Our role as caregivers is always to do what God asks us to do and to leave our reputation up to Him. It doesn't really matter what our family and friends think about our volunteering. It doesn't really matter what others who *don't* volunteer may think of us. What matters is this: Are we doing what we truly believe God has directed us to do? If so, He's also in charge of the consequences.

I have encountered people who do not believe they have the right personality for volunteering. I like to explore what people who use this excuse see as the "right" personality for lay ministry. And I do my best to convince them that God likes people of *all* personality types and can certainly use people of *all* personality types.

There are others who are simply reluctant to step forward or be in the limelight. Some who are hesitant may fall into the category of "not comfortable around children." They perhaps have never spent much time with children, although in many cases, I find those people to be very generous toward other people's children. Some of them are among the most amazing aunts and uncles I have ever met.

I quickly assure the more timid people that not every person who has volunteered at Eugene Field felt qualified to mentor children. An interesting phenomenon I've observed through the years is that these individuals—if they are willing to go just once to the school—often become very faithful volunteers for many years.

Two such people were June Autry and my niece Michaela Cole Silverberg. I asked them to join me in being Lunch Buddies at the school. We picked up Happy Meals at McDonald's and found ourselves assigned to three third-graders who became our Lunch Buddies. It was not only amazingly easy for each of us to blend into the children's lives, but it was a fun outing that became a meaningful part of each week.

We often played a very competitive game called Connect Four, and occasionally, we spent some of our lunchtime reading with our girls. Mostly, we ate lunch and talked about things the three Eugene Field girls wanted to discuss.

I learned a valuable lesson in this. It is always easier, it seems, for a person to go with another volunteer into a new ministry setting. Jesus' wisdom in sending out His followers two by two still holds!

It was easy for those who were Lunch Buddies to take part in the birthday party celebrations held quarterly in the Youth and Family Center gymnasium on the First United Methodist campus.

At the birthday parties, the children had an opportunity to skate on the center's hardwood floor and to enjoy birthday cake and pizza and receive an armful of gifts and party favors. The years passed quickly, and before we knew it, our three girls were going to the fifth-grade graduation party and then moving on to middle school. (At that time, Eugene Field served grades K through 5; then the school changed to grades K through 6. Beginning in fall 2015, the school again served grades K through 5.)

One of the amazing things to me is that June is still in touch with her Lunch Buddy. Her "little girl" is making an adult life for herself in another state, but she takes time to visit with June when she comes back to Oklahoma to visit family and friends. June is learning to relate to her as an adult friend, a young woman she was blessed to watch grow up, face tough problems in life, and display amazing resiliency.

Real Fears. There is yet another category of excuse that can create a reluctance to volunteer: a very real, frightening experience in the proximity of the caregiving site.

I believe that virtually *every* ministry faces periodic bouts of fear—either an experience involving a ministry leader, champion, or member of the volunteer ministry or a threat against those who are being mentored. For that matter, even a church leader who suddenly faces budgetary or personnel concerns without any apparent solution can feel fear related to volunteer ministry. We feel very blessed that we have had very few of these fear attacks at First United Methodist, but we are also very aware that they can and may happen.

One of our volunteers preparing to become involved in the Anchorhold ministry experienced a personal bout with fear. He was bitten on the shoulder by a dog while hiking in an urban wilderness area several miles away from where he intended to become involved in ministry. The attack was completely unprovoked, and his physical wounds healed well. But he couldn't seem to shake the feeling of fear that he felt in the aftermath of the dog attack. When he saw the same breed of dog running loose up the street where the Anchorhold house was located, his fear increased.

This man and his wife met with the first Anchorhold director at First United Methodist, Tom Hoffmann, who encouraged them to *embrace* the fear with an eye toward identifying more fully with their neighbors. He suggested they begin to pray specifically for their new neighbors who were battling fear, which Tom assured them was likely in a neighborhood that had as much social upheaval and poverty as the greater Epworth neighborhood. He reminded them that many people in our society today live in fear daily, and those who don't know Christ really have no reprieve from that fear. Furthermore, he reminded them that Christ said that His perfect love flowing in and through them would be the key to casting out fear.

That one conversation with Tom Hoffmann led to a change in perspective and not only gave this man and his wife the courage to continue their work at the Anchorhold residence but also to see the dispelling of fear as a major goal in their conversations with their neighbors.

This man's experience gave *me* a new insight as a minister to lay ministers: Whatever we have had as an excuse for ministry probably is related to some type of inner fear. It is as we confront that fear that we have a new foundation on which to become a minister to someone the Lord is likely to send our way—someone who struggles with the same fear and excuse in life. Rather than seeing any attribute as *disqualifying* a person for ministry, I choose to see every experience as *qualifying* a person in a unique way.

Excuses about Time and Resources. Countless people, of course, use the excuse of "no time" or "no resources" for their failing to volunteer for ministry. Many say, "I'll volunteer later. I just can't right now."

While I certainly acknowledge that there are legitimate reasons for not being able to volunteer at the present time for a lay ministry, I also know that *nobody* has enough time or enough resources. We all feel stretched most of the time.

Some people do need to work two jobs. Some people do have extremely heavy workloads in caring for elderly parents at the same time they are raising young children. Some people work at careers that tap into their caregiving skills and energy (from clergy to social workers to healthcare workers).

But … I have also learned these two things:

One, everybody has the same number of hours in a day, and everybody has something he or she can give as a resource if the will is there to give. The issue is not one of lack, but rather, priority.

Two, most of the people who use time resource excuses have rarely spent time talking to the Lord about *His* desires regarding their work in lay ministry. I encourage them to do so.

Staying Involved, Remaining Persistent

My second major role as the minister of community ministries is to encourage volunteers to *stay active.*

Below are several points I make in many of my periodic presentations to volunteer groups.

1) Don't neglect your personal devotional life. Stay in the Word, and, very importantly, keep praying.

The supporting structure for all genuine Christ-honoring ministry within our church, and elsewhere, is the Word of God. It is from God's Word that we must draw our understanding of God's vision and how to implement it—not only His universal vision for all believers in all places at all times but also His very specific vision for each of our churches, ministry groups, and individual lives. God's Word has clear directive for issues great and small.

The Bible has numerous examples of helping that is *beneficial* and of helping that can result in *hurting.* The Bible has even more words of advice about what we are to do for others—both fellow believers in Christ and nonbelievers—and what to expect as we reach out with God's love. We are wise to root all of our efforts in the fertile soil of God's wisdom.

The application of God's Word, however, is *always* enhanced by prayer. Prayer calls us to focus our attention and to activate our behavior. Prayer calls us to see ourselves in the *context* of God's current plans as well as His eternal purposes.

Let me point out several ways in which prayer and God's Word go together.

First, prayer opens our own minds and hearts to invite the Lord to plant His vision into our lives—both individually and as a group of like-minded volunteers in His church. There is great benefit from reaching agreement with others that what we are about in terms of giving and serving is not ultimately *our* man-made idea, but *God's* idea. There is great benefit in realizing that the Lord is inviting us to participate in His ministry on this earth and that He delights in our willingness to be His hands and feet in practical serving.

We benefit always when we see that God does not deal with us in a heavy-handed top-down insistence on ministry; rather, in the vast majority of cases, He *invites* us to be co-participators in the miracles that He is developing and implementing in our immediate world. He *invites* us to be in His vineyard.

Furthermore, the Lord delights in our inviting *Him* to be our Lord—in very practical and specific ways, directing what He would like for us to do, when, with whom, where, how often, and with what attitude and goals. Something special happens when we invite the Lord in prayer to use us for His purposes—to pour Himself into us and through us and to anoint our effort. We become more malleable in the Spirit. We become more willing, even eager, to do His bidding. We become more aware that our service is a privilege because it is an extension of the tremendous privilege we have of being in intimate relationship with Him.

The Lord delights in our inviting *Him* to be our Lord— in very practical and specific ways, directing what He would like for us to do, when, with whom, where, how often, and with what attitude and goals.

A pastor once told a group of people who were part of a new members class: "At some point, I am going to disappoint you as your pastor. I apologize in advance for that. At some point, however, you are also going to disappoint me. We can experience great sadness, and perhaps even dissolution of our relationship, if we allow ourselves to dwell on our disappointments. How do we avoid this? We must both keep our eyes on the Lord and our ears attuned to His directives. We must see ourselves in direct relationship with Him and accept that He has an amazing ability to work *all things* for our good and His glory. That includes our mistakes, foibles, personality flaws, and sins of both omission and commission. If we will cling tightly to the Lord, trusting Him to be at work in all things at all times, we will not be disappointed. Rather, we will be delighted and experience new bursts of spiritual growth and blessing."

How true!

Second, ongoing prayer makes us more sensitive to the Lord's transformative process in our own lives. To this end, it is helpful to keep a journal related to one's volunteering. I encourage our volunteers: Make notes about what you perceive the Lord is doing, how He is inviting you to be a servant to others, and what He is doing within your own heart. How is your thinking changing? How is your attitude changing? How is the Lord watering your own creativity to produce new approaches or methods—and in what ways are you becoming a more effective volunteer in ministry? There is great reward, and ongoing motivational energy, in seeing that God is at work *in* us as well as *through* us.

Third, prayer builds our faith to take greater God-directed risks in ministry—to say what we might otherwise not have said or to reach out in tangible expressions or in ways we may have been too shy or reluctant to try.

The more we fuel our ministry efforts with prayer and faith, the more rewarding the volunteer work is likely to be—and the greater the results we are likely to see. We begin to learn that the most effective forms of ministry are those that truly are reflections of the Lord's own character traits and His earthly ministry. Yes, He *does* call us to preach the good news, to help those in bondage to be set free, to teach His benefits, to encourage others to hope again, and to experience God's healing and wholeness in every area of life!

When this happens, we are far more likely to lay aside our own agendas and to be vessels that pour out *compassion* to other people even as we develop a *passion* for Christ Jesus.

Step by step, as time passes, we become people who no longer do things *for* others, but do all things *with* others as people who are walking with other people on a journey of the Lord's choosing—walking with both those we serve and those who are our fellow volunteers.

There are countless opportunities to pray for and with those who receive our caregiving. Although our work at Eugene Field is in a public school and therefore subject to laws related to the active sharing of faith, there is nothing that prohibits a volunteer from praying for students in the volunteer's private prayers. And in my experience with the school, I don't know of any instance in which a volunteer has been reprimanded for praying with a student who *requested* prayer.

Many of our volunteers have been asked by the children at the school, "Why are you here?" The answer, of course, is twofold: "I am here to help you do well in your schoolwork, and I am also here to pray for you anytime you want me to pray." When given that open door, students have frequently felt very free to ask their mentor to pray about something in their personal life or the life of a sibling or parent.

The children at the school, of course, are not the only ones who face difficult life situations. One volunteer once told me that she was sitting in the hall with her mentee when a teacher stopped and whispered to her, "Please pray for me. I am really struggling." The volunteer was quick to pray! Later, she learned that earlier that day, this teacher had a student in her classroom who experienced a major seizure; shortly after that, another student was escorted from the school by police because of an outburst in the classroom, and then, within the same hour, her husband had called to say he had lost his job!

The volunteer could do nothing but pray, but she discovered that prayer was exactly what was needed most.

On another occasion, this same volunteer was approached by a child at a community dinner. The child said, "My mother wants you to pray for her." The volunteer was surprised at the request and even more surprised to discover the mother could not speak English. She had been unable to sleep, at night, and her prayer need was for *sleep*. The volunteer took the woman by her hand and prayed fervently as her young daughter translated the prayer for her mother. At the next community meal, she heard the good report—the woman had been able to sleep well ever since that prayer time.

Moments like that may seem small, but in the life of a person in need, they loom large and can be catalysts for a lasting change in attitude and faith.

We have seen many answers to prayer, not all of them answered in the way we thought they might be. For example, a volunteer named Faunelle Deaton would from time to time go with Emily and Don Renberg for prayer walks through the school corridors and around the playground. There was a large tree on the playground that had been cut down but the stump remained, and that was a favorite place for them to pray. They routinely prayed that the school would be a safe place where children could learn and feel at peace. They prayed for the children's mental, physical, and emotional needs to be met. At the end of the prayer time, they often said, "Lord, if there is anything that is not of You, may it be removed. Amen!" And then they'd go for ice cream.

One morning, Faunelle got a call from Emily to give her advance warning about an article that was in the morning newspaper. The headline screamed the bad news: "Tulsa School Teacher Removed from Teaching after Solicitation Charge." And there, embedded in the article, was a less-than-flattering photo of one of Faunelle's favorite Eugene Field teachers. She had always regarded him as a special teacher, someone who put in extra time and effort with the children and was always concerned that each child be clean and have clean clothes. The children in his classes really learned, and they scored well. Faunelle, Emily, and Don were relieved to discover that the man's arrest did not involve children, but the event was both troubling and sad for them. Then they remembered, "Didn't we ask God to remove anything from the school that should be removed?" They could see that God had indeed answered their prayer.

Volunteer ministry is always an opportunity to see God work in unusual ways. I remind our volunteers that our role is to pray whenever God leads us into that opportunity. His role is to use our prayers in the way He desires. We may never see the fruit from our prayers, but we can be confident that God is using and will use our prayers in ways that He orchestrates.

2) Explore inwardly what God may be doing.

A volunteer who becomes discouraged very often sees a lack or failure in the tasks of mentoring or lay ministry as the source of his or her discouragement. I find that my best response is to remind the person to look at what

God may be doing in the volunteer's own life—not in the life of the mentee or ministry recipient.

We must always look for signs of our own spiritual growth!

A volunteer may begin with a concern for how he or she might help others, including how the lay minister might impact the spiritual growth of others, but very quickly, those who volunteer in neighbor-to-neighbor ministries discover that the fruit of spiritual growth is the work of the Holy Spirit in all who participate. The lines become blurred between givers and receivers, the "helpers" and the "helped," the servants and the served.

A teacher once reminded me that every good teacher readily admits that he or she learns more from the teaching process than the students. That is also true when it comes to volunteerism. The volunteers are enriched and impacted as much or more than those who receive their gifts of time, talent, and care.

Rather than looking outwardly for change, look inwardly. What is God doing in *your* life, and how does this relate to your work in ministry? You are *His* mission field even as others are *your* mission field.

3) Choose to stay in the relationship.

All relationships are transformational. We are changed by the relationships we develop in life. There is nothing theoretically magical about volunteering. Volunteers give their time, knowledge, service, and energy for one main reason: to develop a *relationship* with others that will be meaningful to both parties. The relationship, given to God as an offering, becomes the fertile ground for growth, development, and true transformation.

Ultimately, no volunteer *changes* a student, a homeless person, a neighbor, or any other person being served. *It is always God who does the changing*, and even as God may change the person being served, we can always count on God to change the one who seeks to serve.

4) Remain hopeful.

Hope is a choice.

Romans 12:9–13 is one of my favorite passages in the New Testament. In his admonition to the believers in Rome, the apostle Paul calls for them to "Let love be without hypocrisy. Abhor what is evil. Cling to what is good. Be kindly affectionate to one another with brotherly love, in honor giving preference to one another, not lagging in diligence, fervent in spirit, serving the Lord; rejoicing in hope, patient in tribulation, continuing steadfastly in prayer; distributing to the needs of the saints, given to hospitality."

I can't think of a more succinct set of marching orders for any volunteer or a better overall command for any volunteer organization.

I am especially drawn to the phrase "rejoicing in hope." In one translation, this phrase is "happy in your hope." Dr. Tim Bias, former General Secretary of the Board of Discipleship of the United Methodist Church, has turned HOPE into an acronym standing for Hospitality, Opportunity, Purpose, and Engagement. I join him in believing that if those four facets are present in a volunteer ministry, there will be plenty of optimism and joy!

Hope, of course, is always biblically tethered to heaven. The concept is rooted in lasting values and the best kind of blessings, and the assurance of eternal rewards even if immediate blessings are not readily evident.

I encourage our volunteers often: "You may not see the full harvest of the seeds you plant. Plant anyway! God sees, and God grows a harvest that will amaze you one day." I believe that wholeheartedly.

13

Looking Toward the Future

Can there ever be too many volunteers for effective lay ministry in a community? I doubt it. There will always be a need for more people and for new volunteers to replace those who move away, die, or are no longer capable of serving in the ways they once served.

There will always be a need to raise up the next generation of volunteers—those to whom we will pass the baton of caregiving.

And there will always be the need for an infusion of new energy, fresh new ideas, creative approaches, and the enthusiasm that seems especially strong in the newly recruited. New volunteers give old volunteers the opportunity to pass on their wisdom and skills as well as the historical perspective of the ministry. I see a healthy diversity of ages as desirable in every area of lay ministry.

Needs also tend to change and evolve over time, but this does not mean they are eliminated or fully met. Rather, there is a need for new methods and protocols.

Yes, there is always a need for more volunteers—and that means there is always a need to

- Tell others what has been done,
- Tell others what is being done, and
- Tell others what might be done if they help!

There is always a need to recruit younger people.

There is always a need to involve new members in the old familiar programs.

There is always a need to say thank you to volunteers, to acknowledge their efforts and successes, and to share the practical tips they have learned through their research and applied experience.

There is *always* a need for more thanksgiving, praise, and prayer within the volunteer camp.

Halftime Volunteers

I am eternally grateful for the day I first heard about Bob Buford and his *Halftime* book and the related event-based program he developed. Buford, perhaps more than any other individual I know, has been a catalyst for launching countless ministries among people who know what it means to *build* successful organizations and *organize* volunteers. Many of these ministries are the result of people attending the Buford weekend conferences and becoming part of Halftime communities. The founders of the new ministries that are forged under the Halftime umbrella or influence are very often former CEOs, business owners, nonprofit leaders, and others who had very profitable and experience-rich "first half" years of their life but who are now ready for a new challenge that might move them from "success" to "significance."

In 2001, I found myself in Nigeria on a mission trip at the time of the 9/11 attack on America. I was traveling with people who were as shaken by that experience as I was—but who, like me, saw it as a wake-up call that God still had more for us to do in our lives and more people for us to serve in ministry roles.

Several weeks before 9/11, I had recruited a group of members at First United Methodist to go with me to a Leadership Network conference in California shortly after my return to the States from Nigeria (I have routinely taken laity with me to conferences such as this, believing it to be important for them personally and also for the church). It turned out that Bob Buford was holding a Halftime luncheon as part of the conference, and the Lord sovereignly arranged for us to wander into that luncheon, where we were made to feel very welcome—and from which we left changed!

Halftime conferences are designed primarily for those who are entering a "second phase" of life. For some, it is an empty-nesters phase, for others retirement, for others a second career.

At a Halftime event, participants are invited to

- Identify the passions that God has developed in them
- Determine how the person desires to be most helpful to others
- Identify the group of people to whom the person feels drawn

Participants are encouraged to identify their doubts, questions, and fears—most importantly, those doubts, questions, and fears that are keeping them from genuine spiritual growth and service.

The goal of those involved in Halftime ministry is to help people discover God at work in the midst of their daily life and to learn to trust the Word, the Holy Spirit, and the body of Christ to lead them into transformation that generates even greater purpose and fulfillment in life.

Most of those who attend these events come away renewed and ready to take risks to discover the "something more" they believe is still there for them to be, do, and experience. The key method for transformation is nearly always identified as "service."

Bob Buford challenges people with five critically important questions:

1. What am I really good at?

2. What do I want to do?

3. What is most important to me?

4. What do I want to be remembered for?

5. If my life were absolutely perfect, what would it look like?

An honest and thorough exploration of those questions—and a coming to answers through diligent and humble prayer—has a proven track record of moving a person from "good years" to "the best years of your life."

I am continually searching for those in our church body who are approaching retirement. I often say to them, *"You are now ready for volunteering! What has God been preparing you to do?"*

Buford, of course, does not want any person to wait for retirement to become a volunteer or become more active in ministry. The time to begin those efforts is *years* before retirement. It is when a person is in his forties, and certainly by the early fifties, that a person must already be exploring, learning about, and engaging in volunteer ministry that is fulfilling. Yes, and a thousand times again, *yes!*

If you are in church leadership, I encourage you to be very proactive in your recruitment of those who are in the forty- and fifty-year-old age range. Many people in this age range are empty nesters. Others are beginning to question how they want to finish out a career path. Some are in the so-called midlife crisis. Volunteering in ministry is a great cure for those who are experiencing middle-age problems, especially feelings of diminished worth, unreached dreams, changes in routine, and loneliness. There are causes to be pursued and needy people to be helped. Those who actively seek to give in new ways are going to find that they receive far more than they can ever give.

Growing from Strength to Strength. The Bible refers to God's people growing "from strength to strength" and "from glory to glory."[1] Halftime is all about this type of growth. It is not for people who need motivation nearly as much as it is for people who are reprioritizing their lives and redirecting their motivation.

Many of those who come to Halftime events do not feel unhappy. A high percentage have good marriages, a degree of success in their career, and a degree of security and cushion that enable them to take enjoyable risks and pursue fun adventures that often have a ministry component. At the same time, many of those who attend admit, "I wasn't unhappy, but I also wasn't fulfilled." They have an itchy feeling in their souls that there is still something *more* that God wants them to do and to become.

This does not mean uprooting all of the past and trading it in on a radically different future. In some cases, perhaps. In most cases, there is a sense of renewed self-discovery, of putting more of the pieces of the life puzzle together to see things a little differently and adjusting priorities in a new way for greater purpose and the opportunity to exert greater influence. Some have a burning desire to win souls, others to encourage the saints, and still others to teach, preach, heal, or pursue very practical ministries that engage in such activities as digging water wells, feeding the hungry, and bringing social justice to people who feel left out or put down in their world.

Our Halftime Community. When we returned home from our first exposure to Halftime, Clark Millspaugh and Bruce Riddle led the way in the formation of a Halftime community at First United Methodist. Clark became our Halftime champion.

We sponsored several events to introduce others in our church to the Buford concepts. These meetings also gave us an opportunity to share and explore specific ministry ideas that God was giving to us and to feel mutual support from others who were also seeking to experience greater significance and greater results in their walk with the Lord.

In many ways, Clark fit the ideal profile of a successful Halftimer.

The basic message of the *Halftime* book and the groups it spawned is that a person should take the profits and the many career-related contacts they amass during the first half of their careers and use that money and network to make a difference in the world during the second half of their active life. The challenge is for participants to put their money where their mouth is—or perhaps more accurately, to put their money where their faith lies. Clark had been a very successful businessman in Tulsa, and he had solid financial relationships and close friendships with dozens of people in the greater Tulsa area. He brought many of these people into service at Eugene Field.

Joe and Pat Lee were also Halftimers at First United Methodist. They had a second home in Colorado, and they began to use this ranch for ministry purposes. They hosted a number of couples from the church for times of rest and rejuvenation. They believed in our Eugene Field ministry and hosted a mentee from Eugene Field on a retreat to the ranch. There was always a strong spiritual component embedded in their hospitality.

Dave and Clydella Hentschel were yet another Halftime couple. Dave was an oil company executive in his "first half" career, and Clydella had been heavily involved in United Way fundraising. Giving had been a part of their lives. After they became a part of the Halftime community at First Methodist, the Hentschels became involved with our outreach at Eugene Field. They volunteered at our community dinners, serving the residents. They also helped send Clinton Middle School students to the Wyldlife camp. After Clydella passed away, Dave remarried, and he and Susie continue broad financial outreaches into the community. Dave and Susie continue to support community dinners and the Christmas baskets for Eugene Field families. The Christmas baskets are a much-anticipated facet of the holiday season.

Looking back, I can also see clearly that Emily and Don Renberg, so critical to our becoming involved at Eugene Field, were Halftimers—they just didn't know it. They had left a successful business career to devote themselves to volunteer service—not at retirement, but in the prime of their lives.

Recruit Volunteers of All Ages

We believe it is God's plan for us to recruit volunteers of all ages and to give responsibility for a great deal of creative decision-making to our volunteers, perhaps especially to young volunteers.

A few years ago, a young parishioner heard a sermon about community ministries and the thought occurred to her, *I could paint little girls' fingernails.* Taylor Sanders acted on her idea, recruited her longtime friend at church, Emily Charles, and they developed a plan to paint the fingernails of young girls who were hospitalized, hoping to make them feel loved, pretty, and special. They called their idea "Pretty as a Princess." They put together a PowerPoint presentation and printed flyers to recruit other young women to their cause. And then they ran into a serious snag.

The hospitals all required volunteers to be fourteen years old. Taylor and Emily were only thirteen.

As you might have anticipated, I was quick to recruit them for a ministry at Eugene Field. They held their first after-school event in September 2013, and later expanded their outreach to include book readers, music leaders, and craft facilitators to join the fingernail painters.

The "Pretty as a Princess" participants were matched in small groups of four younger girls with two older girls (eighth-grade volunteers). The girls met after school over crafts, stories, music, and nail polish and talk about a wide variety of topics—as girls tend to do!—from school, friends, and princes, villains, and ball gowns.

For more than two years, Taylor and Emily spent five to seven hours a week preparing for and running their "Pretty as a Princess" ministry. In keeping with their ministry theme, the girls recruited their mothers to be "Fairy Godmothers." After all, somebody needed to drive their Cinderella coaches to and from Eugene Field.

Involving Entire Families

A second key group of people to target for volunteer ministry is families with children older than eight but younger than college age. My message is: Get them involved in what *you* are doing. Make volunteer ministry a family affair.

At First United Methodist Church, we have a tradition of organizing our Sunday school classes according to a set of factors that primarily include age and interest. Those who come together to form a class name their class, and each class is challenged to find ways of enjoying friendship outside the church walls and beyond Sunday classes and also to find and adopt a particular ministry that members of the class might do together.

Through the decades, a number of parents from First United Methodist have taken their children with them as they volunteered behind the scenes at Eugene Field Elementary School. There are children at our church who grew up helping sort inventory for the Big Bucks Store, weed plants in the Global Garden, and help their parents wrap and pass out gifts.

In recent years, one Sunday school class developed a program called "Sunday Is Funday" at Eugene Field. The Fundays were held several times a year. At a Funday, groups of students move through a variety of activity stations. The children of the First United Methodist Sunday school class members interact with the Eugene Field children on these days, with older siblings preparing meals, supervising the various art projects and gymnasium games, and providing individual attention in reading activities and board games.

Another class has hosted an Easter egg hunt for Eugene Field children. Again the children of this class's members joined their parents in face painting and other games and craft projects, interacting with the Eugene Field students while gaining a sense of what it means to volunteer in ministry.

What a wonderful heritage this is for a child! And what a tremendous source of new life for a church and its outreach ministries through the years!

I recommend to you Bob Buford's book, *Halftime.*

ENDNOTES

1   2 Corinthians 3:18; Psalm 84:7.

14

Lessons Learned

At First United Methodist Church:

- We work very hard to have something that *everybody* in the church can do in outreach ministry to our greater community.
- We encourage church members to develop their own ministries in areas of their particular skill or passion.
- We have a wide variety of ways that people can contribute to a ministry at a wide variety of levels.

If there could only be three lessons to pass on to you as a volunteer or a minister to volunteers, those would be the lessons.

There are other vital concepts that have framed the *way* in which I have led community ministries during the last two decades. I also offer those lessons learned for you to consider and to adapt in ways that are most useful for your purposes and in your environments.

Three Ways a Faith Institution Interacts with a Community

The book *Communities First*, edited by Jay Van Groningen, identifies the following three ways in which faith institutions traditionally interact with communities.[1] For easier communication, I substitute the word "church" for "faith institution." I have found these concepts very helpful in giving volunteers a framework for evaluating their ministry roles.

1. **IN *the Community.*** The church does not desire to influence its surrounding community; most of the resources of the church are invested in programs that benefit its own members. The church leadership and members may see themselves as a "fortress" holding back the outside world's evil influences. While the church campus may take up space in the neighborhood, the members tend to commute to the church from other neighborhoods and return to their own neighborhoods after services or meetings. The church does not pay taxes and in some ways is

a net drain on the community, doing little to provide jobs to community members, contribute to public schools, or provide access to the church's auditoriums, spaces, or landscaped yards.

2. **TO** *the Community.* The church desires to bless its surrounding community and make contributions to it, but on its own terms. There is very little desire to have the community involved in the decisions made by the church. Some resources are spent in the community, usually a small percentage of an annual budget. There is little contact with the community to generate ideas about ways in which the church and community might interact—the church serves the community with methods it prefers, for reasons it has chosen, and with an assumption that the church intuitively knows what is best for the community according to its own evaluation criteria. Many of the gifts, skills, and resources in the community are overlooked. The church sometimes shares its space with the community—performing programs and services to which the community residents are invited to participate (sometimes for a fee and sometimes for free). The church tends to have a neutral presence and influence.

3. **WITH** *the Community.* The church desires to influence the community and to be involved with representative members—ideally, the leaders—of the community. It spends significant resources (time, talent, money) in the community. It looks for ways to utilize the gifts, skills, and resources that already exist in the community. It uses planning and assessment processes that are recognized by both church and community participants and makes decisions that consider the impact on the community as well as on the church. The church seeks to have a *transformational* impact—change and growth for both church members and community residents and business owners. The church sees itself as a servant to the community, adding value to the residents and the community as a whole. While it does not pay taxes, it nevertheless is a *contributor* to the community.

Beginning to Work *With* a Community. There are several steps that make working *with* a community smoother and more effective.

First, someone within the church must have a vision for what the relationship might become. In most cases, the church building, campus, or physical plant is already in existence, and there is a legacy of some type in terms of the way in which the church and community have interacted in the past. If the church is a new plant, there is going to be a set of opinions about what other churches have done in the past and a certain perspective in the community about what *any* church is likely to want to do.

We need to recognize going in that shadows and ghosts lurk within the church and the community. It will take a mutual desire to work *together* toward good goals for a church to truly be able to work *with* a community.

Second, someone needs to call a prayer meeting or a prayer initiative. There needs to be some process that acknowledges that without divine help and approval, no efforts are going to succeed, at least not to the level that most participants might want. Nothing that is truly *transformative* occurs without the Spirit of God hovering over the chaos and creating new life.

Ideally, members of the church and the community will come together to pray. Practically speaking, much of the prayer required is likely to occur in other venues. Either way, there must be a mutual awareness among church members and community residents that the ensuing relationship will be one in which God is respected as the ultimate Author and Finisher.

Third, there may be need for a statement of some kind that becomes a sign-on starting point for mutual cooperation that leads to mutual growth and development. This might be as simple as an exchange of letters between the church pastor and the perceived leader of the community (elected or non-elected, formal or informal). It is important for both the church leadership and the community leadership (one or more people) to seek a good *relationship*.

Good relationships are marked by:

- Open communication, free flowing and frequent
- An attitude of conciliation that seeks peace, mutuality, cooperation, relationship—and in some cases, reconciliation of old wounds or misunderstandings
- Mutual humility—no one group knows it all or has it all
- A desire for growth and development that is positive and beneficial in identifiable ways for both parties

Fourth, representatives of both groups—church and community—need to meet together with a clean slate. An ongoing dialog needs to begin, lasting as long as necessary for there to be both consensus and *enthusiasm* for taking on mutually recognized needs with mutually recognized goals and methodology.

Insights into Ways to Engage a School of Your Own

There are likely as many ways to adopt or volunteer at a school as there are churches or volunteers within a church. Here are my top 20 suggestions, many of which correspond to the Lewis Center's "50 Ways to Engage Local Schools"[2]:

1. Learn about schools within a four- to five-mile radius of your church. Drive through the areas. Study the basic demographics.

2. Meet with the principal or school volunteer coordinator. If you are going to establish a relationship with the school, you *must* have a key administrator's support or approval. If possible, have conversations with teachers, area social workers, coaches, and even the school nurse to get a sense of the school's most pressing needs. Overall, make this visit—or visits—without a set agenda. Go on a fact-finding mission with your main question being, "How might we help?"

3. Take your "dream team" to the school. Ask a small group of volunteers who have expressed an interest in helping a school to go with you to visit the school and observe what is happening there. The people in this group will likely see things you didn't see and have impressions you may not have had on your visit.

4. Answer the question, "Is somebody already helping?" If so, don't try to reinvent the wheel. Explore the opportunities for partnering with those who are already volunteering, or move on to a place of identifiable need with a lack of volunteers. Explore ways you might serve alongside others who are already volunteering.

5. Prepare your volunteers with sufficient training. Conduct appropriate background checks. Help your volunteers gain a strong understanding about what they can and cannot do in the school. Place an emphasis on student safety and relational boundaries. Prepare your volunteers to be in full compliance with the school's volunteer guidelines and be sensitive to all church/state boundaries.

6. Invite people individually. Start small and grow. The Bible teaches us never to despise the days of small beginnings (see Zechariah 4:10).

7. As opportunities arise, attend school activities to help develop relationships with teachers, students, and parents. Sometimes the best opportunities are outside the class—showing up at school events and big games, student concerts, PTA meetings, and fundraisers.

8. Under-promise and over-deliver.

9. Be committed. Stay the course. This is especially important in one-on-one tutoring and mentoring relationships built between volunteers and students.

10. Pray for the school's administrators, teachers, students, and their families.

11. Keep current with local education issues and needs. Don't rely solely on media reports. Ask the principal if there are problems you need to know about or issues that may impact the work of your volunteers in the near future. Attend the open board meetings of the school district to see what's being planned.

12. In your efforts to provide supplies for students (such as school uniforms, stocked-with-supplies backpacks, or winter coats, hats, socks, and mittens), conduct your giveaway times with dignity and respect. Be generous and caring, never condescending.

13. Seek opportunities to celebrate the success of students and teachers, whether the "success" is a birthday, career milestone or anniversary, or community recognition. Be quick to praise students to their teachers and to praise teachers to their principal. Be genuine in your praise— point to success that is verifiable and respected.

14. Speak positively at all times. Even in debriefing sessions, point toward what has been accomplished or what *might* be accomplished. Put the emphasis on good performance and outstanding potential.

15. Recognize that students in need are usually from families in need. Explore with your church volunteers ways in which your church might help with these greater needs in the neighborhood of the school.

16. Always be on the alert for answers to the "why" questions—*why* does this need exist, *why* hasn't something been done already, *why* is the Lord calling *us* to this place to address this need, *why* doesn't money solve everything?

17. Be a strong advocate for public education. It *is* worth greater excellence. Stay up to date on the decisions and work of the local school board. Speak up if doing so will have a positive impact, and stay silent if speaking up may cause harm. Ask the Holy Spirit to give you good discernment.

18. Recognize that too much top-down giving or decision-making from outside the school community can hinder more than help. Some "help" truly is toxic. Don't become a purveyor of it.

19. Be a voice for hope. And whenever possible, also be a voice of faith.

20. Expect transformation. Don't be surprised when you succeed at certain things. Rejoice, and keep working. There's always a new level of excellence to pursue.

Make the Time for Periodic Reflection

I heartily encourage all community ministry directors and leaders of volunteer groups to take the time and make the effort to periodically reflect upon and discuss the ministries that are in place, including a conversation about what the future of those ministries might look like.

Note the words *time* and *effort* above. We must be intentional about these reflect-and-discuss times or they will never occur.

I offer these five words below to you for interaction, discussion, and brainstorming:

1. *Transformation* (a deep process of change)

2. *Relationship* (which can always be risky but can also lead to greater trust and transparency in communication)

3. *Partnership* (genuinely working together with shared effort and mutual humility)

4. *Reconciliation* (with Christ and with people)

5. *Vision* (long-term and short-term goals, dreams, direction)

Ask about each of these:

• How might this be *Spirit* led? How can we know what God wants?

• In what ways does our current ministry activity reflect these five attributes? How have they developed over time? Where might we go from here?

An Intentional Reevaluation. There are things we are wise to look at in a direct and intentional way:

The Big Picture. First, we must step back to look at the big picture. It is all too easy to become embroiled in the daily chores and schedules of volunteer work. It is also easy to fall into a practice of measuring activities and volunteer efforts with numbers—the number of people involved, the number of dollars spent, the number of service hours, the numbers related to scores that show improvement and growth or decline and loss, the numbers that reflect the level of appreciation or participation on the part of those being served, and so forth.

Four Major Questions to Ask. Four questions must be considered from time to time when it comes to the purpose of a volunteer ministry:

1. *Is our mission statement still our mission statement?* It is amazing to me how some groups move away from their reason for being and never seem to notice that they are no longer doing or pursuing their founding purpose.

2. *Is it time to stop an area of service—and if so, why?* Does this intent to cease operations actually mean the morphing of that area of service into a new form of service or perhaps the blending of the existing activities of two different volunteer ministries into one larger ministry (for better coordination of people, resources, funds, and impact)?

3. *Is God calling for an expansion or the creation of a new level or degree of outreach?* Perhaps more people are in need of being served. Perhaps there's a new dimension of service that needs to be added. Perhaps there's a new way to infuse practical service with a greater spiritual message.

   Of equal importance are answers to these questions: Who is determining the new direction or new level? Is it the church leadership, the volunteer ministry leadership, the volunteers, or those who are voicing increased need?

   Growth solely for the sake of added numbers—numbers of volunteers, numbers of dollars, numbers of people served—is never the best way to go.

   The old saying is still true: "What God commands, God equips."

   When God is calling a group to do more, give more, be more, proclaim the gospel more (and more effectively), then God will provide the resources necessary to get that job done. If people simply want a bigger platform or more authority or a higher profile, God does not necessarily climb on that bandwagon and send it to the head of the parade.

4. *Is Jesus still the leader of the ministry or outreach?* We don't like to admit it, but there are many organizations that begin as evangelistic or

discipling ministries that degenerate into social clubs. As one person once said, "Jesus went missing."

The Ultimate Evaluator. In the end, the only true criterion for evaluation must be: "Is God pleased?" The answer to that question leads us to ask, "How can we know with assurance that God is pleased?" "What more might we do to bring Him greater pleasure?" "Are we truly doing what He has asked of us?"

We must never conclude that we *can* know or calculate the full effects of our service to others. Only God sees the full impact of our work and the full purpose He has for us *as* we work. He alone knows the beginning from the ending of any mission or ministry activity.

We are stuck in time. God's plans and purposes are eternal. It is good to remember that we may catch glimpses into God's eternal harvest even if we never experience a great deal of that harvest during our tenure of volunteering.

As for a way to evaluate whether God is *pleased* … There is much to be said for "feeling the pleasure" of the Lord as we do our work. It seems highly likely that this ongoing sense of the Lord's pleasure is the greatest delineator of God's will for the volunteer.

A person once said, "When I serve my neighbor, I have a sense that God is looking on around the edge of an open door and *smiling.*"

If we don't have a sense that God is pleased, we need to step back and take another look at our own attitude in serving, our own ways of displaying God's love to the ones we are serving, and our own expectations for personal recognition or reward. Those are difficult things to do—and are things that often require the discerning abilities of others around us. Asking the question, "Is God pleased?" is always a good place to begin a discernment process and to evaluate one's feelings of purpose and fulfillment.

If volunteering becomes drudgery, emotionally painful, or filled with conflict, there's very good reason to stop and ask, "What's going on?"

The best answer is not rooted in logistics, personality conflicts, or financial or time restraints. The best answer is likely in the realm of spiritual fruit-bearing. We are made for growth. We have been created to pursue spiritual fulfillment. We are made to reflect God's joy. When growth, fulfillment, and joy fall away, we need to go to the Lord for answers as to "why" and "what now."

This is not to say that a volunteer can escape at all times a sense of boredom, a routine that becomes too predictable, or a sense of futility born of too-few results. At times, it is not the volunteer activity that is the root of the problem but rather other relationships, circumstances, or events that are competing for the volunteer's spiritual time and energy. It is good to recognize those impingements.

It is also good to recognize that every form of volunteer ministry must have a degree of creativity reserved *for the volunteer*—nothing should be so prescribed as to become a straightjacket of performance.

We also must recognize if and when a person becomes burned out at the volunteer tasks he or she has been doing and if and when a particular activity has run its course. Perhaps the volunteer has done all that he or she is capable of doing or has been designated by the Lord to do. Perhaps the job is done.

We must also be on the alert for changing environments and circumstances that may signal a new situation that requires increased or expanded prayer and discernment. Is the volunteer program under new spiritual attack? Is the problem one that must be addressed through spiritual warfare before practical results can be realized?

All are good questions to ask.

All are a part of stepping back to regain a new sense of the big picture from time to time.

Exploring New Goals and Agendas

When we ask, "Is the agenda changing?" we are never to look at a ministry as a *thing*. It is a group of *people*. It is alive. It is organic in its design, with few defined edges and shapes. It does not function like a machine. It functions always as some semblance of *family and friends*. Everything that is organic—that is a living entity—has a time and season for its establishment, growth, and development.

A changing agenda can also mean a step up or a step back from existing goals. This might include a changing scope for a volunteer ministry or a change in the sharing of responsibilities.

It is very helpful for those involved in a volunteer ministry to acknowledge and accept these two basic principles:

First, God Is the Boss. Every volunteer must have a sense that he or she has been recruited into a particular area of service by the Holy Spirit—and that the Holy Spirit will equip, guide, and motivate the volunteer if the volunteer is willing for Him to do so.

This is not only a principle that a volunteer must acknowledge but also a *supervisor* of volunteers.

A leader of a volunteer ministry cannot *force* a volunteer to work. A leader of volunteers can only *motivate* a volunteer to serve. That motivating process is nearly always limited to encouragement, appreciation for all levels of effort and giving—small as well as great—recognition of service, applause for accomplishment, and ongoing communication that nurtures and affirms. It is the role of a leader to ask, "What is the Lord doing in your life? How are you feeling about your work as a volunteer? In what ways might I do more to support you with my prayers?"

Nothing motivates a volunteer quite as much as hearing the phrases, "Well done!" and "Thank you!"—both in private conversations and group settings.

It is also very beneficial for the leader of volunteers to periodically conduct volunteer-only events that are aimed primarily at the spiritual refreshment of the volunteers. The event might be a one-day retreat, an overnight retreat to a local monastery or conference center, a party just for volunteers, or some other type of event that makes the volunteers feel special, encourages them to trust God for their energy and rewards, and calls attention to the efforts, time, and results of volunteer service.

Our church recently held a luncheon for volunteers in one area of ministry. The church paid for the meal. A special speaker addressed the *spiritual* nature of the very practical volunteer work being done, and the senior pastor was present to lead the meeting and give his recognition to those in attendance. It should not be taken lightly that "a good time was had by all," or that six months later, people were still recalling the words of encouragement given to those invited to attend.

Second, God Is the Empowerment. Not only does the Lord *call* a person to volunteer service or a church to a volunteer-based ministry, but the Lord *empowers* those He calls.

Not long ago, I heard about a church that had remodeled a couple of "temporary" structures into a unified building that included a worship sanctuary, a kitchen, a nursery, and two Sunday school rooms. The church was eager to have a series of potluck lunches after Sunday services to welcome visitors and build a sense of fellowship at their new location.

It wasn't until the building was completed, however, that the women of the church were invited to take a look at the limited kitchen facilities. They discovered only two electrical outlets—far from adequate for plugging in crock pots and electric casseroles to keep potluck dishes warm during the morning service before lunch!

Every volunteer ministry of any kind needs times of refreshment and empowerment. There must be an opportunity for volunteers to "plug into" the ministry.

Three methods of empowerment are readily achievable:

First, there is empowerment that comes from involvement and association. People enjoy gathering together with others who are involved in their choice of ministry—sharing stories, laughs, concerns, and generally feeling part of what is being done or experienced. Volunteers are by nature "groupies." Few people are motivated enough to maintain ongoing and consistent service in solo ministries—volunteers are people who need other people.

Second, there is empowerment in information. Volunteers need updates about what is happening, what has been accomplished, and what is being planned for the near and more distant future. They need to be able to look *back* and feel pleased at their involvement in a ministry, look *around* and be encouraged that lives are being impacted and improved, and look *ahead* with enthusiasm for new opportunities to share and celebrate the Lord.

Information is nearly always presented best in a group setting—face to face, perhaps with handouts or a short PowerPoint presentation. Testimonials from those who have benefited from a ministry can be very motivating.

Third, there is empowerment in shared thanksgiving, praise, and prayer. We thank the Lord for what He has done, is doing, and has promised to do—in us and through us as individuals and as a collective body of volunteers. The greater the flow of thanksgiving, the greater the awareness will be regarding God's faithfulness, direction, and presence.

We praise the Lord for who He is—His everlasting and ever-present attributes. The greater the flow of praise, the greater the awareness of God's goodness and His desire to bless all activities that reflect His love, mercy, and tender kindness.

On the basis of a faith that is renewed by thanksgiving and praise, we petition the Lord very specifically.

We voice our concerns—not as a means of informing the Lord (surely He already knows all needs and opportunities), but rather to affirm that *we* are aware of our need for Him and His presence as we undertake our opportunity to serve. We ask for His guidance, provision, and ongoing strength and energy to do the tasks ahead and, above all, for an outpouring of His love, that we might do all things in the Spirit of Christ to bless others.

Beginning and ending meetings in prayer is just the start. There should be an ongoing atmosphere that prayer is appropriate at all times in the "doing" of a ministry—it should never be considered inappropriate to stop for a quiet, private moment of prayer to ask for the Lord's wisdom, answers, and assistance. It should never be considered a strange phenomenon to give thanks or praise.

Thanksgiving, praise, and prayer *empower* a ministry spiritually and empower the individual volunteer in ways that nothing else can.

Show me a ministry that has plenty of places for volunteers to plug in for camaraderie, information, and spiritual nourishment, and I'll show you a ministry with eager and faithful volunteers!

Bits of Practical Advice.

- Schedule volunteer meetings at times when most people can attend. There are various times on any church calendar that are better than other times—discover them. You may need to have more than one meeting; if so, schedule the meetings close together, perhaps on back-to-back days.

- Keep your volunteer meetings short and focused. You may not need to have a printed agenda for others, but do have an agenda written to guide your own leading of the meeting.

- Schedule your volunteer meetings on a regular basis, holding open the possibility for emergency meetings if necessary. In my experience, regular meetings with volunteers tend to defuse the need for emergency meetings.

- Keep your supervisor and other ministers informed—not only of the meeting(s) but also of the information and ideas covered in the meetings. Information needs not only to flow up and down an organizational chart, but horizontally. There's good reason to coordinate efforts and avoid duplication of ministry service as well as to avoid duplicate bookings of facilities, resources, and personnel.

- Accept the awards your church may be given as a way of encouraging your volunteers.

  First United Methodist Church has been honored in a number of ways for its partnership with Eugene Field—here are a few: the Governor's Conference on Oklahoma Partners in Education in 2002; the Stacey Roggendorff Partner of the Year Award in 2004; the Tuskoma Brown Miller Award for Human and Civil Rights from the Oklahoma Education Association in 2006; the Partnership in Education Investing in the Future Award in 2009; the Outstanding Faith-Based Partner Award for Large Congregations from the Tulsa Regional Chamber Partners in Education in 2013; and the Partnership in Education PSO Public Service Award for longevity in 2016. We have been grateful for the recognition, but we are even more thankful for the opportunity to collaborate with these community groups.

- Seek to have goals that require faith to reach. In spite of our two decades of involvement and the work of literally hundreds of volunteers from First United Methodist Church, we still haven't reached our goal—to have one adult mentor linked to every student at Eugene Field Elementary School. We still haven't *fully* reached our greater community for the Lord. We still haven't given our best to our defined corridor. We're on our way, but we haven't arrived, and we still work to recruit more and more volunteers! We continue to pray for God's direction.

Finally ...

Choose a verse for your lay ministers that becomes synonymous with your understanding of all outreach to others—both within your church and in the community. I encourage you to find your own verse, but until you do, I offer you mine:

> "Let your light shine before others, that they may see your good deeds and give glory to your Father who is in heaven." (Matthew 5:16 ESV)

These questions beg to be asked:
In what ways do you need to turn on your light?
Where is God directing you to let your light shine?
I pray God's blessings as you answer these questions and then live out the answers.

An excellent resource is The Lewis Center for Church Leadership at Wesley Theological Seminary in Washington, D.C. This organization is a great resource for those who are seeking to impact their communities through involvement with local schools. The Lewis Center offers videos, presentations, and supplemental materials. Here are some of the foremost titles they have for video and narrated presentations:
- Why Schools Matter to the Church
- The Power of Doing What Matters
- Discerning a Vision for Supporting a Local School
- Supplying Student Needs
- Supporting and Affirming Teachers
- Helping Students Succeed
- Developing a Heart for the Needs of Children and Schools

A number of Lewis Center DVDs and CDs are available in downloadable formats. Check out their website: http://churchleadership.com/resource/default.htm
Email contact: lewiscenter@wesleyseminary.edu

ENDNOTES

1   Jay Van Groningen, ed., *Communities First* (Grand Rapids, MI: Christian Reformed World Relief Committee, 2005), 9-10.

2   "50 Ways to Engage Local Schools," Lewis Center for Church Leadership, accessed April 2, 2014, lewiscenter@wesleyseminary.edu

Appendix

Timeline for First United Methodist Church of Tulsa Involvement with Eugene Field Elementary School

Year	
1995	First Methodist adopts Eugene Field as a "Partner in Education" Back-to-school fashion show (raised funds to start the Big Bucks Store) Big Bucks Store opens "First Friends" mentor program established Teacher/staff Christmas party
1997	Chess Club Fun Fair Summer Academic Buddies
1998	Bicycle Club Birthday parties Touch a Teacher Cherish a Class (volunteers acting as homeroom moms)
2002	Craft Club Garage sales Sewing Club (Hearts & Hands Together) Parent-Teacher Conference Incentives program
2003	Fifth grade graduation Community dinners
2005	Alphabet Club (to help kindergarteners learn their ABCs) Fifth grade celebration with fishing Kanakuk Kamps scholarships
2007	Global Gardens Uniform drive
2008	Shepherd's Fold Ranch (scholarships to summer camp)

2009   Uniform drive
         Bicycle Club
         Birthday parties at YFC
         Bible clubs
         Harvest Market opens

2010   Wyldlife Camp for Eugene Field graduates
         Christmas for two classrooms
         Wednesday night dinners (in cooperation with West Tulsa United
            Methodist Church)

2011   Teacher Appreciation Dinner
         Burgh Church Resource Partnership
         Family Fun Fest/Hullabaloo

2012   Sixth grade graduation
         Sports Camp and Upward Basketball (scholarships for seventy-six students)

2013   Sixth grade graduation event
         Pretty as a Princess
         Community dinners in partnership with Growing Together and
            Harvest Community Center
         Reading Partners collaboration

2014   Partnership with Contact Mission Christmas Store
         After-School Bible Club

2015   Celebration for Leader in Me and Honor Roll students at YFC
         Eugene Field Volunteer Reunion celebrating 20 years of partnership
            with Eugene Field Elementary School
         Family portraits

This is not a comprehensive list of ministries at Eugene Field during the last two decades. Rather, it is a representative list of the types of volunteer work given from the church to the school. A number of Sunday school classes and church families have assisted with donations of food, clothing, personal items, and gifts on an as-needed basis, often as one-time contributions.

The specific programs developed as various volunteers gave them definition. I believe this is a critically important point to make—we did not "design" our ministry at Eugene Field and then seek out people to implement a church administrator or school administrator plan. Rather, we presented needs and gave volunteers an opportunity to create ministries in which the volunteers felt fully vested and to which they might remain committed over time.

This does not mean that we were disorganized—to the contrary. We adopted a mission statement that has served us well through the years:

> "Our mission, in the love of Christ and His divine power, is to meet the children's academic, social, and spiritual needs through example, demonstration, and prayer—praying for God's encouragement, guidance, and strength to minister to the children, the children's families, the teachers, and support staff."

Ministry Area Map Key

❶ First United Methodist Church of Tulsa
❷ Eugene Field Elementary School
❸ Westside Harvest Market / Global Gardens
❹ West Tulsa United Methodist Church
❺ Epworth United Methodist Church / Anchorhold House

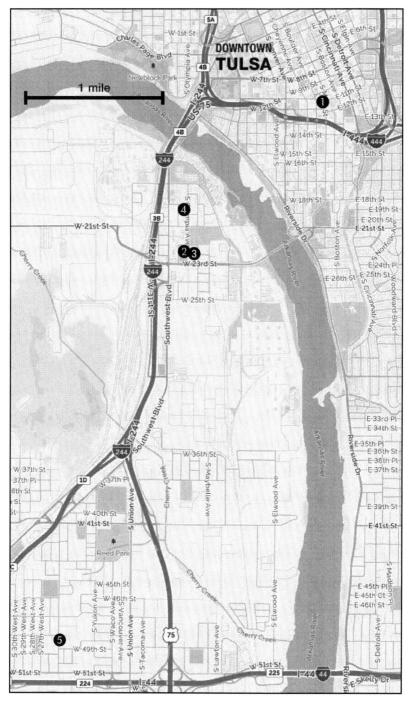

Made in the USA
Charleston, SC
31 July 2016